To mum

Happy cooking

Love
Annette + Jenathan
x x

SIMPLY HOT POTS

Brimming with creative inspiration, how-to projects, and useful information to enrich your everyday life, Quarto Knows is a favorite destination for those pursuing their interests and passions. Visit our site and dig deeper with our books into your area of interest: Quarto Creates, Quarto Cooks, Quarto Homes, Quarto Lives, Quarto Drives, Quarto Explores, Quarto Gifts, or Quarto Kids.

Text © 2019 by Amy Kimoto-Kahn
Photography © 2019 by Quarto Publishing Group USA Inc.

First published in 2019 by Race Point,
an imprint of The Quarto Group,
142 West 36th Street, 4th Floor,
New York, NY 10018, USA
T (212) 779-4972 **F** (212) 779-6058
www.QuartoKnows.com

Race Point titles are also available at discount for retail, wholesale, promotional, and bulk purchase. For details, contact the Special Sales Manager by email at specialsales@quarto.com or by mail at The Quarto Group, Attn: Special Sales Manager, 100 Cummings Center, Suite 265-D, Beverly, MA, USA.

10 9 8 7 6 5 4 3 2 1

ISBN: 978-1-63106-567-5

Photographer: Julia Vandenoever
Project Editor: Erin Canning
Managing Editor: Cara Donaldson
Food Stylist: Nancy Zamparelli
Prop Stylist: Nicole Dominic
Cover and Interior Design: The Quarto Group
Page Layout: Sporto

Printed in China

SIMPLY HOT POTS

A COMPLETE COURSE IN JAPANESE NABEMONO AND OTHER ASIAN ONE-POT MEALS

Amy Kimoto-Kahn

AUTHOR OF *SIMPLY RAMEN*

Race Point
PUBLISHING

CONTENTS

PREFACE

I was born and raised with my two older siblings in Fullerton, California, in Orange County. My sister, Kathleen, and brother, Scott, are the book-smart ones. I, on the other hand, took the more social route and spent time pretending to have my own cooking show in our backyard rather than studying. My love of cooking came from watching my mom throw fabulous dinner parties with her friends; as I got older, I practiced her techniques and cooked for friends and family on my own. I'm not a professionally trained chef, but I've been cooking for more than thirty years. My mom shared her love of cooking with a close group of female friends, and together they created original recipes and hosted elaborate dinner parties, all while managing their own careers and raising children. They call themselves The Dames. Their story—and the reason I have such a passion for sharing good food (and really just throwing a good party)—should be told.

I'm a *yonsei*—a fourth-generation Japanese-American. My parents were both born in California. My mom, Yvonne, is from San Francisco, and my father, Hayato, is from Los Angeles. In 1941, just two months after the Japanese bombing of Pearl Harbor, all people of Japanese ancestry in the United States—be it 100 percent or 1/16th percent—were forced into internment camps. It's not talked about in American history a lot, nor is it part of the core curriculum taught in schools today, but two-thirds of the more than 120,000 people who were interned and accused of being potential Japanese spies were American-born citizens, just like my parents. Both my parents and their families were given ten days to pack up only what they could carry and leave their homes.

My mom remembers the years immediately after her family was released from Amache camp in Colorado. People would throw rocks at her and her sister and brother and call them "Japs"—an ethnic slur after the war. Money was tight. My grandmother went to work as a seamstress, and my grandfather eventually went to work for the same Japanese import-export business he had worked for before the war. They grew vegetables in their garden. My mother and her sister learned how to cook and stretch their available food for days. Fried rice, considered a Japanese peasant dish made from leftovers, was a family staple.

My father suffered similar prejudice after the war, with people spitting at him and calling him names. His family returned to the rougher area of East Los Angeles, where they were able to continue to operate their garment business. My grandfather had been a chef in San Francisco before the war, so he made Japanese dishes such as sukiyaki and shabu-shabu, even though his specialty was meringue cookies. My Auntie Alice sacrificed going to college to work with my grandmother, so the family could

The Dames (My mom is in the second row, far left.).

afford for my dad to attend the University of Southern California. It was there, while studying to be a pharmacist, that my dad met and fell in love with my mom, who was at USC for dental hygiene.

During my parents' time in college, there was still postwar prejudice, and they were excluded from joining social groups, such as sororities and fraternities. It was at USC that my mom decided to form her own group with her female Japanese-American friends, and thus, The Dames came to be. They were the Martha Stewarts of their time. They married, had children, and hosted elaborate gourmet evenings with menus including both Japanese and American dishes. The parties were hosted at different homes and the theme changed for each party. I have such clear memories of helping set the tables with fine china and silver, assisting Mom at the kitchen counter and chipping in with the dishes. It was an initiation of sorts.

Without realizing it, I had absorbed so much information from Mom and her friends that they still, to this day, inspire how I cook for my family and friends. I remember having lemon sorbet for the first time and learning it was not, in fact, a dessert, but a palate cleanser between courses. That early taste memory was the inspiration for my Yuzu Citrus Sorbet (page 157; I definitely encourage you to have it for dessert). I learned quickly that in Japanese cooking, it's very important to "eat with your eyes." In our culture, food presentation is just as important as preparation. I learned to make colorful dishes that were pleasing to look at and delicious. The Dames taught me that sometimes the finishing touch was garnishing a dish with a sprig of heavenly bamboo from our garden or adding a gardenia and some greenery to a dessert tray. When you looked at the food spread across the table, it made you feel special, like you were part of a secret club eating at one of the nicest restaurants in town.

While working on my first cookbook, *Simply Ramen*, I started gathering ideas from a cookbook The Dames wrote back in 1992. It is such a testament to their time (you'll find baby back ribs next to beef shabu-shabu) that it's now sold at the Japanese American National Museum in Los Angeles. The recipes are easy to follow with accessible ingredients and a perfect amalgam of Japanese and American cultures. In that book, I explored and highlighted both traditional and nontraditional ways of making ramen. *Simply Hot Pots* follows this same format, giving you the foundation to make traditional Japanese *nabe* (hot pots) with twelve basic broth recipes and also embracing international explorations of hot pots. Some recipes use a classic Japanese broth, but it might be put to use in a modern way, such as my Slow-Cooked Beef Brisket Tomato Nabe (page 90)—an ode to my Jewish mother-in-law.

I am so pleased to be able to continue to share family recipes in this book along with recipes graciously developed and given to me by friends. Some of my favorites include my friend Emily's juicy and tender Kurobuta Pork Nabe Mille-Feuille (page 69), my decadent but simple Kobe Wagyu Beef Sukiyaki (page 89), my friend Kiko's traditional Chanko Nabe (Sumo Wrestler Hot Pot, page 82), and my visually stunning Crab Legs with Spicy Tonkotsu Nabe (page 114).

Please join me on my continuing journey to preserve my family history through food, and thank you for letting me show you how to make nabe in your own home. Although I may not know you personally, we are now connected through food. Enjoy!

—Amy Kimoto-Kahn

INTRODUCTION

What is hot pot cooking? It's about bringing people together. It's comfort food. It's healthy, affordable, quick, and easy. It's a complete one-pot meal that can be customized for anyone. Hot pot cooking embodies Japanese culture with its use of fresh, seasonal ingredients, delicate presentation, and the humble manner in which it is served. In Japan, hot pots are called *nabemono* (nah-beh-mo-no), or *nabe* for short. The stout, clay, lidded pots that nabe are cooked in are called *donabe* (doh-nah-beh; directly translated, nabe means "pot"). They have not changed in thousands of years and continue to be a fixture in today's Japanese kitchen.

A typical hot pot meal in Japan would have a family gathered around the dining table with a donabe of bubbling dashi (broth) as the centerpiece. There would be overflowing plates of thinly sliced beef, bite-size squares of creamy tofu, fresh *shungiku* (chrysanthemum leaves), and piles of Napa cabbage, tender shiitake mushrooms, colorful carrots, and julienned scallion—all ready to take a short dip in the warm broth. A small bowl of zesty ponzu sauce would be served on the side as a dip for the meat and vegetables. The meal would end with a *shime* (she-meh), or end-of-meal course. After the meat and vegetables had been eaten, a pile of plump udon noodles would be placed into the broth and simmered until warm and brimming with the dashi's delicate flavor. Conversation might slow as everyone sits back, slurps their noodles, and feels full and satisfied.

Although the majority of recipes in this book are Japanese-inspired, hot pots are found all over parts of eastern Asia—from Thailand to Malaysia. I've included a few of my favorites to show not only the versatility and universality of this type of cooking, but also because I'm a huge fan of the international broths filled with aromatics and herbs. You'll quickly find that once you master the fundamentals and Anatomy of a Hot Pot (see page 19), it is easy to experiment within these recipes and make them your own, whether it's using what's in your refrigerator, playing with protein choices, or amping up the heat in your broth to your liking. For each recipe, I've chosen a broth with proteins and vegetables that I think pair well, but you will soon realize these recipes are merely templates. *Simply Hot Pots* gives you the foundation to make traditional Japanese nabe with twelve basic broth recipes while also embracing international explorations of hot pots. There are sauces to go alongside the hot pots, plus some traditional (and nontraditional) side dishes and desserts.

I cook with traditional Japanese ingredients as much as possible, but out of necessity, I also use what is readily available where I currently live in Boulder, Colorado. I want my cookbook to inspire people to learn more about Japanese cooking and culture, and not be intimidated by ingredients they can't find, or techniques that seem unfamiliar or

Donabe

too challenging. Since my family and I moved from the Bay Area in Northern California, I have found the availability of Asian and Japanese ingredients to be a bit more limited. When I was developing recipes for this book, I really put thought into substitutes for ingredients that can be found in most grocery stores or online, so you can still make the recipe even if you can't find the ingredients in your area. If you are lucky enough to live near an Asian market or a Japantown, use it as a cultural adventure to seek out the best of what's in season or take your kids and educate them on the many different types of basic hot pot ingredients, such as mushrooms, tofu, greens, and noodles.

For my family, hot pot nights are when we're excited to come to the table to share our day with each other and cook together, as everyone picks what they like and adds it to the donabe. My hope is for you to do the same with your family and friends.

EQUIPMENT

One of the benefits of hot pot cooking is that you probably already have everything you need in your kitchen already. Nabe cooking is not pretentious—it's casual and more about bringing people together. If you don't have a traditional donabe, use what you have, be it an enameled cast-iron casserole or a deep skillet. If you find that you really enjoy hot pot cooking, treat yourself to a clay donabe later. These glazed pots come in many different styles, so take your time looking for one that is special and speaks to you. While hot pot cooking is not about having state-of-the-art equipment, there are a few utensils, gear, and cooking vessels I will describe—both traditional and nontraditional—that will help you achieve the best results.

Donabe

This is the traditional Japanese clay earthenware commonly used for hot pots and to make stews, steam vegetables or rice, and roast meats. The special clay used to make a donabe conducts heat evenly throughout the surface of the pot and retains that heat even when the temperature is lowered, keeping food warm for a lengthy period.

All donabe come with a lid that has a hole to let steam escape, which also helps regulate the heat. The special clay of a donabe also helps the heat build slowly, which keeps food from burning. Hot pot cooking is all about slowly building flavor over time. They are best used over an open flame on a gas stovetop or a portable gas burner. The flames surround the bottom of the donabe and build heat evenly. (Donabes should not be used on an electric or portable electric stove to avoid uneven distribution of heat.)

When looking for a donabe, a handcrafted one can last a lifetime. Look for one made with coarse clay that has been fired twice. Get one that suits your family's size or entertaining habits—I personally like the larger 4-quart (3.8 L) ones because they are big enough to feed my whole family and any extra guests. My favorite donabe is one I purchased at Toiro Kitchen, a great online shop for donabe ware. It's the large Mushi Nabe and comes with a steamer attachment. I like its versatility—I can cook rice and steam vegetables, as well as prepare hot pots. Plus, it's big enough that I can easily cook nabe for up to eight people.

To prolong your donabe's life, it needs to be cured. The naturally porous clay has small holes that must be sealed to prevent leakage and excessive cracking. This process, called *medome*, involves cooking rice in water until the starches fill the microscopic pores of the pot—this not only helps prevent breakage and damage by heat, but also prevents smells and stains from food that might permeate into the pores of the pot when cooked. Unlike a wok or cast-iron skillet, you do not want the donabe to take on the flavors of the contents cooked in it. Here's a simple method for curing your donabe:

1. Prepare a mixture of about 80 percent water to 20 percent short-grain Japanese rice. (The amounts will vary depending on the size of your donabe.) Add water to the donabe until it's filled about three-quarters full. Add rice to about one-quarter of the water's height. Gently rub together the rice and water with your hands until the water looks milky. Do not drain the water.

2. Cover the donabe and place it over medium-high heat. Bring the water and rice to a slow boil. Remove the cover, reduce the heat to low, and simmer for 1 hour to 1 hour and 30 minutes, stirring occasionally, until most of the water has evaporated and the rice looks like a paste.

3. After this paste-like consistency is achieved, turn off the heat and let cool for about 1 hour and 30 minutes. Discard the rice mixture. Rinse and dry the donabe. It's now ready to use.

Electric Hot Pot

Cast Iron

Electric Hot Pot

An electric hot pot is a great alternative to a donabe for the modern family. It's best used when you are making hot pots with tableside presentation—where meat and vegetables are arranged on platters for guests to cook at the table. Electric hot pots also have an adjustable temperature control so the heat can be easily regulated throughout the cooking process. I own the Zojirushi Gourmet 1350-Watt Electric Skillet, which is a nice large size, but also light enough to store and remove from the cupboard easily.

Cast Iron

Cast-iron casseroles, skillets, or enameled cast-iron braisers, such as Le Creuset brand, are great for hot pot cooking, because they distribute heat efficiently like a donabe. The only downsides to keep in mind are that cast iron gets hot more quickly than a donabe and it doesn't retain heat for as long. They also don't have a lid with a hole, but the same function can be achieved by placing the pot's lid a little askew to allow steam to escape. They are still a much better alternative to stainless steel, which does not conduct heat as evenly or protect your food as well from burning.

Split Hot Pot

I've only been able to find aluminum split hot pots; I do not believe there is a clay donabe that has a split option. That said, these are great when you want to offer both a spicy and a nonspicy version of a base broth, like in my Mongolian Broth (page 53).

Rice Cooker

If you own a rice cooker, you know how essential it is. It makes cooking rice easy and fail-safe, giving you light, fluffy rice every time. Most rice cookers also have a warming function, so you can make the rice before your company arrives, and it will be hot and ready to eat when you need it. In my opinion, Japanese models are superior because they have more settings to choose from specifically for Japanese rice, such as regular white short-grain rice, sushi rice, semi-brown rice, and porridge settings. I'm a big fan of the Zojirushi brand. We eat a lot of rice in our home, so we have the 5½-cup (1.3 L) capacity, but they are available in smaller and larger sizes.

Split Hot Pot

Rice Cooker

Pressure Cooker

Portable Burner

Sieves

Pressure Cooker

If you plan to make your own bone broths—and I strongly encourage you to, as the quality is incomparable—you'll need a pressure cooker. This special pressurized pot makes the process easier and faster. I've found that a 30-quart (29 L) pressure cooker yields about 3 quarts (2.9 L) of rich, unctuous bone broth. You can purchase a smaller model (that will take up less space), but this is a project that requires an afternoon, so you might as well make enough broth to freeze and last a while. The other option is to use an Instant Pot or other electric pressure cooker and make your bone broth in two or three batches, or make the broth in a large stockpot and cook it over low heat for 15 to 20 hours.

Portable Burner

Donabes should not be used on an electric stovetop to avoid uneven distribution of heat and scorching your food. They are best used over an open gas flame, so the flame can surround the bottom of the donabe and build heat evenly. If you plan to serve nabemono tableside and have guests help themselves, a portable gas burner is very convenient. I like the Iwatani 35FW Portable Butane Stove because it's fairly compact and you can set it directly on a wood table without fear of it causing any damage. I recommend buying extra butane cartridges, but one cartridge will last through two to three hot pots.

Sieves

A couple of fine-mesh sieves are must-haves for hot pot cooking so guests can retrieve their protein and veggies from the broth easily. Because a dipping sauce is often served with hot pots, you want the food to be free from liquid so it can soak up all the flavor of the sauce(s) without diluting it.

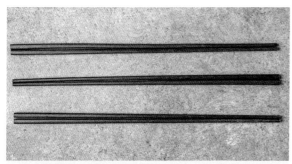

Serving Chopsticks

Platters

Sharp Chef's Knife

Serving Chopsticks

Long chopsticks allow people to sit around the table and add food to the hot pot themselves, even when not within easy reach of the broth. Longer chopsticks allow guests to do this without standing up, and it makes it easier to put food into and take it out of the pot.

Sharp Chef's Knife

If you cannot find frozen presliced shabu-shabu–style meat (very thinly sliced meat—⅛ inch, or 3 mm, or thinner) at your Asian market or have your butcher slice it for you, a sharp chef's knife is essential for slicing the meat at home. The trick is to freeze the protein for up to 4 hours, until it is firm and easier to slice. If you are slicing fish, just refrigerate it overnight until firm. I prefer the forged steel blade of a Japanese knife because it retains its edge longer. Shun is a great brand widely available in the United States.

Platters

Use any large platter, be it round, oblong, or rectangular, for setting your table. A mixture of platters creates a beautiful presentation, so don't feel that they all need to match. I like to separate my meats and seafood from the vegetables to reduce the risk of salmonella. Try arranging everything with a variety of color and texture to make it pleasing to the eye.

ANATOMY OF A HOT POT

What makes hot pots so simple and delicious is that they all have the same basic components: a base broth, proteins and vegetables, noodles, and/or rice, garnishes, and sauces. Here, I outline some of my favorites in each category, as well as a description of why each is used. Remember that any recipe can be made with substitutes if you can't find the specific ingredients in your local area (substitutions are in parentheses after the recommended ingredients). I have also included a Hot Pot Glossary (page 164) for your reference if you don't know what some of the ingredients are.

The method for cooking, whether stovetop or tableside, depends on the cooking time for your ingredients. (The preferred cooking method is noted for each hot pot recipe.) If everything being cooked only takes a short amount of time to poach in the base broth, I recommend cooking tableside where the thinly sliced pieces of meat and vegetables only need to simmer for 1 to 2 minutes, like with my Rib-Eye Beef Shabu-Shabu (page 91). If you are cooking larger pieces of chicken with thicker pieces of kabocha (Japanese pumpkin) and eggplant, for instance, I recommend cooking on the stovetop, like with my Thai Chicken Coconut Curry Hot Pot (page 79). Sukiyaki, a very traditional type of nabemono, can use either of these methods, but I prefer tableside because it's better cooked in batches, as the thin meat requires only minimal cooking time, like with my Pork Sukiyaki (page 70) and Kobe Wagyu Beef Sukiyaki (page 89).

As you learn more about hot pot assembly, you will be able to pick a favorite base broth and then choose your preference from each of the other categories with the method that best suits it. Regardless of the method you choose, what's most important is to enjoy the process and experiment—there is no right or wrong way, as long as you are eating together and taking pleasure in the company of family and friends.

Base Broth

Your base broth is the foundation for the flavor layering that will be fortified by the ingredients that go in it. Traditional Japanese broth is made with dashi, a combination of water, kombu, and bonito fish flakes, but more flavored broths, such as *tonyu* (soy milk) and sesame miso, are also used, as well as more viscous broths, such as a chicken or pork bone broth.

Protein—Poultry/Beef/Pork/Duck/Seafood

Your protein choice can really change the flavor of your base broth. Chicken tends to give it a lighter, more savory flavor; beef, pork, or duck makes it a bit richer; and seafood imparts a salty brininess. I've been lucky enough to find all my proteins in thinly sliced form at Asian markets, so I haven't had to worry about slicing them. My favorite is Kobe Wagyu beef because of how tender it stays regardless of cooking time and how well it pairs with sauces, such as miso sesame.

Udon noodles as the shime (end-of-meal course).

Greens

Greens add color and flavor to the broth, as well as texture variation, and they balance the mellowness of other vegetables. They are great for dipping into sauces. Shungiku (chrysanthemum leaves) and Napa cabbage are my favorite greens and are the among the most popular hot pot ingredients.

Mushrooms

Mushrooms provide a meatier texture to the hot pot, round out the earthier flavors of the broth with their umami goodness, and add a visual balance. I'm a big fan of enoki mushrooms; they are light and delicate, and cook up quickly. If you can find maitake mushrooms, they add a wonderful earthy flavor to any hot pot, and their flowerlike appearance makes them one of the most beautiful mushrooms.

Onions

From sharp and acidic to sweet and mild, onions play an important role in hot pots, because their flavor and texture change with the length of time they are cooked. Guests can choose whether they want a crisper texture with more bite and flavor or a mellower taste, blending with other ingredients. I prefer *negi*, or Japanese green onions, to any other onion because, when raw, it flavors the broth with a strong onion taste, but as it cooks it becomes milder and sweet, making it easy to eat in large amounts without being overpowering.

Roots/Tubers

When roots and tubers are cooked just right, they have a nice al dente feel to them. They pair well with proteins and make a hot pot heartier to satisfy your guests without making anything too heavy. I always cook these for less time because they can easily overcook and get mushy. I like kabocha, or Japanese pumpkin, because you can eat the peel and it tastes like both sweet potato and pumpkin.

Vegetables

Easy to add, veggies can really change the flavor of the broth, based on what you use. They balance the color and texture, and contribute the best of what's in season.

Tofu

Loaded with protein and nutrients, tofu is a star ingredient and one of the best for soaking up the flavors of the broth. Different varieties are becoming more available in supermarkets, which makes it easy to incorporate into your cooking. A firm silken tofu is my choice for hot pots because it has the creamy, melt-in-your-mouth texture of silken tofu but the firmness to retain its shape and hold up better when being handled with the rest of the hot pot ingredients.

Rice

Not just a filler side dish, steamed Japanese rice can be one of the best accompaniments to make a hot pot go from good to great. The quality of rice can vary greatly, so look for a higher-end brand. *Haiga* rice, which is like a combination of white and brown rice, is one of my favorites for hot pot cooking because it has a delicious nutty flavor and really soaks up the broth when used for the shime (end-of-meal course).

Noodles

Noodles are a great addition to hot pots because Japanese varieties come in gluten-free and low-calorie options that won't deter anyone from a seat at the table. They are either added to the pot directly or can be eaten as the shime. Udon noodles are very filling and soak up and get coated with the broth—these are my choice for the shime.

Garnishes

Garnishes are dependent on what goes well with the main protein and vegetables being served. I always provide *shichimi togarashi*, a Japanese spice-blend condiment. Other condiments include *sansho* pepper powder for extra spice; thinly sliced scallion; grated daikon (Japanese radish); minced chives, garlic chives, or garlic flowers; toasted black and white sesame seeds; and shredded nori (seaweed).

Sauces

The most traditional Japanese sauces are ponzu and sesame, but other international hot pots have a wide variety of sauces ranging from chili oil to peanut sauce.

Eggs

With Japanese hot pots, it is traditional to use a beaten egg as a dipping accompaniment to sukiyaki. Many restaurants cannot serve raw eggs, so it is not always provided. Raw whole eggs can be placed in hot pot broths to slowly cook until they are soft-boiled.

COOKING NABE

The daily routine at my house is pretty casual, so nabemono is our favorite way to cook. Nabe in Japan is just that—a simple and humble dining experience shared with your loved ones. The style of food offered for nabe can range from relaxed and comforting to more elevated and refined, and the same goes for the tableware. If I am entertaining special guests or have relatives in town, I will pull out my favorite porcelain dishes for nabemono; however, you should never worry about having the most expensive china or the most ornate donabe. The simple, colorful display of vegetables and proteins on the table makes the presentation special and beautiful on its own.

Whether entertaining or enjoying a casual night at home with my family, there are a few basics that I always follow when setting my table for nabemono. These aren't complicated or hard-and-fast rules, so feel free to adapt these general guidelines to what suits you.

Setting the Table

I prefer eating nabe tableside because I like the activity of watching my family select what they want to cook for themselves, and I'm tricked into feeling like I'm getting a little break from cooking. There are hands crossing, people dipping, conversation happening—it's almost a bit chaotic, but in the best way.

Depending on the type of service (tableside or stovetop), the dining table should be set with a portable gas burner, electric hot pot, or hot plate for the donabe in the center. If you are cooking tableside, you'll see guests' eyes open wide and their mouths start to water when they see the bounty of food laid out on platters in front of them. They'll want to dig in immediately, so it's good to turn the burner on low and preheat the broth so it is ready to turn up to a gentle boil right as guests are seated. Each table setting should have the following:

- A shallow bowl or a small plate, depending on whether your hot pot has a broth you'd like to pour over the food when it is served.

- If rice is being offered, small, individual bowls with hot, fluffy rice. Fill them right before your guests sit. Place this at the top left of each setting.

- A napkin folded on the left side or tied in a neat knot and placed on each plate.

- Chopsticks in the center above the plate.

- A glass of cold ice water, especially if it is a spicy hot pot. Place it at the top right of the setting.

- Individual serving bowls for sauces. Place them on either side.

Preparing and Serving Nabe

If serving nabe **tableside**, arrange all ingredients on platters. I like to pile each ingredient in a mound on the platter so you can see the contrasting colors. I also recommend separating raw meats from the vegetables, noodles, and tofu, and placing them on different platters. Any food for the shime (end-of-meal course), such as noodles or rice, can be served at the same time as everything else. Place these platters of ingredients on either side of the donabe before cooking. Offer any garnishes, such as fresh herbs or seasonings, within reach. Also, after years of wiping down a dirty table at the end of the night, I now like to place small plates on either side of the donabe for setting long serving chopsticks, a sieve, and a large spoon. (The serving chopsticks are helpful if you have a long table and someone on the end needs to reach the hot pot, and a sieve is a great way to get all the cooked meat and vegetables out of the broth.)

When I serve a nabe that has been cooked on the **stovetop**, I like to ladle the soup into all of my guests' bowls while they sit at the table. Then I return the nabe to the stovetop or the portable gas burner so it can simmer over very low heat and stay warm. If any of my guests are hungry for seconds, they can help themselves—this keeps the meal relaxed and casual.

BROTH BASES, SAUCES, AND MORE

BASIC DASHI

SKILL LEVEL: Easy · **PREP TIME:** 10 minutes, plus 3 hours soaking time · **COOK TIME:** 30 minutes ·
YIELD: Makes 2 quarts (1.9 L)

INGREDIENTS

**2 pieces (4 inches, or 10 cm) dried
kombu**

**10 cups (2.4 L) room-temperature
water**

**2 ounces (55 g) loosely packed
bonito flakes (about 6 cups)**

In the simplest terms, *dashi* is the Japanese term for stock. It's the basis for a lot of Japanese cooking and can be included in simmered dishes like nabemono (Japanese stews and soups), dressings, and even sauces. If you don't have time to make dashi from scratch, there are instant dashi products that can be decent substitutes. Kombu—edible seaweed taken from deeper in the ocean with more flavor than seaweed taken nearer to the surface—is the main ingredient in dashi. It is best soaked in room-temperature water and boiled briefly. If boiled for too long, the kombu produces a slimy film you do not want in your dashi.

INSTRUCTIONS

1. With a damp cloth, wipe the kombu lightly to remove any dirt, but do not remove the white powdery coating, as this gives the dashi flavor.

2. Fill a large saucepan with the water and add the kombu. Let soak for 3 hours. Remove and discard the kombu.

3. Bring the water to a boil over medium-high heat, then reduce the heat to a low simmer. Add the bonito flakes. Simmer for 10 minutes.

4. Strain the stock through a fine-mesh sieve set over a large bowl; pressing on the solids to extract as much liquid as possible. Discard the bonito flakes.

5. Dashi can be refrigerated for up to 1 week or frozen for up to 1 month.

CHICKEN STOCK

SKILL LEVEL: Easy · **PREP TIME:** 10 minutes · **COOK TIME:** 3 to 4 hours · **YIELD:** Makes 10 cups (2.4 L)

INGREDIENTS

3 quarts (2.9 L) water

1 pound (454 g) chicken wings

1 pound (454 g) bone-in, skin-on chicken thighs

2 large scallions, white and light green parts, halved crosswise

1 tablespoon (15 ml) kosher salt

This chicken stock recipe uses wings and thighs because these dark meat cuts have more fat on them and retain their flavor better for a stock. Rather than discarding them, I like to fry them up in a little bit of oil after making the broth and toss them in some teriyaki sauce.

INSTRUCTIONS

1. Fill a large stockpot with the water and bring to a boil.

2. Add the chicken wings and thighs, scallions, and salt. Return the water to a boil, reduce the heat to low, and simmer the broth, uncovered, until reduced slightly and flavorful, 3 to 4 hours. Skim off any scum that floats to the surface.

3. Remove the chicken and strain the liquid.

4. This stock can be made ahead and refrigerated for up to 1 week and frozen for up to 2 months.

VEGETABLE STOCK

SKILL LEVEL: Easy · **PREP TIME:** 30 minutes · **COOK TIME:** 3 to 4 hours · **YIELD:** Makes 10 cups (2.4 L)

INGREDIENTS

10 cups (2.4 L) water
4 celery ribs, coarsely chopped
2 large carrots, scrubbed and
    coarsely chopped
1 large yellow onion, unpeeled,
    halved
1 package (8 ounces, or 227 g)
    cremini mushrooms, cleaned
1 Honeycrisp apple, halved
1 head garlic, halved crosswise
1 small bunch fresh parsley
4 sprigs thyme
2 bay leaves

This all-purpose recipe is from my colleague Julia Heffelfinger, who's a pro recipe developer and editor. The addition of an apple is her mom's trick; she adds a tart Honeycrisp apple (but really any non-mealy apple will work) for a touch of sweetness to round out the earthy vegetables. Also, this stock is a great way to use up any vegetables scraps. She keeps a large resealable plastic bag in her freezer. Any time she ends up with carrot peels, parsley stems, mushroom stems, apple cores, or onion roots and peels, she sticks them in the bag. When it's full, she dumps it into a stockpot, covers everything with water, and simmers away.

INSTRUCTIONS

1. In a large stockpot, combine all the ingredients. Cover and bring to a boil.

2. Reduce the heat to low and simmer, partially covered, until very flavorful, 3 to 4 hours.

3. Strain the stock into a clean pot. Discard the vegetables and aromatics.

4. This stock can be made ahead and refrigerated for up to 1 week and frozen for up to 2 months.

BASIC SHABU-SHABU BROTH

SKILL LEVEL: Easy • **PREP TIME:** 30 minutes • **COOK TIME:** 20 minutes • **YIELD:** Makes 2 quarts (1.9 L)

TO MAKE IN ADVANCE

Chicken Stock (page 30) or
    Vegetable Stock (page 31)

INGREDIENTS

2 quarts (1.9 L) Chicken Stock or
    Vegetable Stock (or store-bought
    low-sodium chicken or vegetable
    broth)
2 pieces (4 inches, or 10 cm, each)
    dried kombu

I love shabu-shabu–style nabemono because it can only be enjoyed communally and pleases everyone—from my five-year-old to my husband. Shabu-shabu is an onomatopoeia for the sound the food makes when you swish it back and forth in the boiling broth. I giggle every time my kids say "shabu-shabu" while they swish their meat and vegetables around. Traditionally, this gentle wafting of meat is done in water only, and it's the ingredients you swish around in the water that add flavor. My version starts with chicken stock (or vegetable stock) and kombu because I think you end up with a more complex broth. The shime, or finish, of this meal is the best part for me—simmering the delicious leftover broth with hot steamed rice or udon noodles after all the meat and vegetables are consumed. My favorite recipes that use this shabu-shabu broth are the Rib-Eye Beef Shabu-Shabu (page 91) and Seafood Medley Shabu-Shabu (page 99).

INSTRUCTIONS

1. In a 4-quart (3.8 L) hot pot or large saucepan, combine the chicken stock and kombu. Let the kombu soak in the stock for 30 minutes without heating.

2. Bring the chicken stock to a boil over medium-high heat. As soon as it reaches a boil, remove and discard the kombu. (Leaving the kombu in boiling water produces a slimy residue that will make the broth bitter.)

3. Use the broth immediately or let cool and refrigerate until ready to use.

4. This broth can be made ahead and refrigerated for up to 1 week or frozen for up to 2 months.

CHICKEN BONE BROTH

SKILL LEVEL: Advanced • **PREP TIME:** 15 minutes • **COOK TIME:** 2 hours 30 minutes • **YIELD:** Makes 3 quarts (2.9 L)

EQUIPMENT

30-quart (29 L) pressure cooker (read and follow the manufacturer's instructions; if you do not have a pressure cooker this size, prepare this recipe in 2 or 3 batches in a smaller slow cooker or electric pressure cooker, such as an Instant Pot, or make it in a large stockpot and cook over low heat for 15 to 20 hours until the broth is a creamy white color and all the meat has fallen off the bones)

INGREDIENTS

1½ pounds (680 g) chicken wings and drumettes

6 pounds (2.7 kg) , skin-on, bone-in chicken thighs

2½ pounds (1.1 kg) chicken drumsticks

1 pound (454 g) potatoes, unpeeled, cut into large chunks

5 quarts (4.8 L) water

Homemade bone broth has a silkier mouthfeel and gives your hot pot a richer chicken flavor, so if you have the time to make this, your hot pot will be better for it. The key here is using a pressure cooker (or an Instant Pot or other electric pressure cooker if you have one) because the steam inside the pot draws out the bone marrow, giving it an unctuous, slightly thick consistency and a creamy, opaque color.

INSTRUCTIONS

1. In a 30-quart (29 L) pressure cooker, combine the chicken wings and drumettes, thighs, drumsticks, and potatoes. Cover with the water, making sure the total volume of water and ingredients does not exceed half the height of the pot.

2. Place the cover on the cooker, leaving the pressure regulator weight off the vent pipe. Turn the heat to high until steam flows from the vent pipe (this may take up to 20 minutes) and continue to let vent for 10 minutes more while the steam displaces the air in the cooker. Place the regulator weight on the vent pipe and maintain a high heat setting. Start timing your cooking when the regulator weight begins to jiggle or rock. It may appear as if it is leaking, but this is normal. Regulate the heat so it maintains a temperature between a 240°F and 250°F (116°C and 120°C). Start the timer and cook for 1 hour.

3. Turn off the heat and allow the pressure gauge to return to 0 (zero) before gently removing the cover. Push the chicken bones down to press out the fat—this makes the soup thicker and creamier.

4. Return the pressure cooker to medium-low heat. Cook for about 1 hour more, uncovered, stirring occasionally, until the broth is creamy white and all the meat has fallen off the bones.

5. Turn off the heat. Remove all the larger bones. Using a large fine-mesh sieve set over a large stockpot, strain the remaining solids and discard them.

6. This broth can be made ahead and refrigerated for up to 3 days or frozen for up to 1 month.

BASIC SUKIYAKI SAUCE

SKILL LEVEL: Easy • **PREP TIME:** 5 minutes • **COOK TIME:** 10 minutes • **YIELD:** 6 to 8 servings

INGREDIENTS

1 cup (240 ml) shoyu (Japanese soy sauce)

¼ cup (60 ml) sake (rice wine)

¼ cup (60 ml) mirin (sweet rice wine)

¼ cup (50 g) sugar

Of all the nabemono, sukiyaki is the most popular in my family and one of the easiest to prepare. The ingredients are easy to find and the fact that it can be made ahead of time makes pulling the actual meal together a quick—come home from work and make it in 20 minutes—kind of dinner.

INSTRUCTIONS

1. In a small saucepan over medium-high heat, combine all the ingredients and bring to a boil.

2. Reduce the heat to low and simmer for about 5 minutes, whisking occasionally.

3. Transfer to a heatproof jar and let cool. Refrigerate until ready to use.

4. This sauce can be made ahead and refrigerated for up to 1 week or frozen for up to 1 month.

PORK BONE (TONKOTSU) BROTH

SKILL LEVEL: Advanced • **PREP TIME:** 25 minutes • **COOK TIME:** 3 hours • **YIELD:** Makes 3 quarts (2.8 L)

EQUIPMENT

30-quart (29 L) pressure cooker (read and follow the manufacturer's instructions; if you do not have a pressure cooker this size, prepare a half batch in an Instant Pot, but I do not recommend using a regular stockpot for this.)

INGREDIENTS

10 pounds (4.5 kg) pork knuckles or trotters, pounded with a mallet to release the marrow

¼ cup (60 ml) shoyu (Japanese soy sauce)

¼ cup (60 ml) mirin (sweet rice wine)

1 teaspoon kosher salt

1 piece (1½ inches, or 3.5 cm) fresh ginger, peeled and finely grated

½ teaspoon roasted chili oil, plus more as needed (optional)

This unctuous, creamy, fat-laden broth is one of my favorite hot pot broths—it's brimming with depth and layered flavor. This recipe does require a pressure cooker and some patience to break down the collagen in the pork bones, but the preparation is minimal and well worth the effort. Make this broth without the chili oil if you prefer a milder flavor or add it if you like some spiciness.

My sensei at ramen school taught me to pound the pork bones with a mallet to loosen the marrow so it melts right into the broth when you cook it—so don't skip this important step! Pressure cooking the pork pieces compresses the fat and bone marrow, making this broth incredibly silky and creamy in just 2 hours—versus 20 hours on the stovetop!

INSTRUCTIONS

1. In a large stockpot over high heat, combine the pork bones with enough water to cover (roughly 5 quarts, or 4.8 L) and bring to a boil. Cook for 15 minutes, uncovered; drain well. Rinse the pork bones thoroughly to remove any scum.

2. Add the cleaned bones to a 30-quart (29 L) pressure cooker. Cover the bones with water (about 4 quarts, or 3.8 L), making sure the total volume of water and pork bones does not exceed half the height of the pot.

3. Place the cover on the pressure cooker, leaving your pressure regulator weight off the vent pipe. Turn the heat to high until steam flows from the vent pipe (this may take up to 20 minutes) and continue to let it vent for 10 minutes more while the steam displaces the air in the cooker. Maintain a high heat and start timing your cooking when the regulator weight begins to jiggle or rock. It may appear as if it is leaking, but this is normal. Regulate the heat so the weight only jiggles 1 to 4 times per minute. Start the timer and cook for 1 hour.

4. Turn off the heat and allow the pressure gauge to return to 0 (zero) before gently removing the cover. Press down on the pork bones to get all the bone marrow out. Return the pressure cooker to medium-low heat and cook the broth for about 1 hour more, uncovered, stirring occasionally, until it is creamy and milky white in color.

5. Using a fine-mesh sieve set over a 4-quart (3.8 L) hot pot or large saucepan, strain the broth, pressing on the solids to extract as much liquid as possible. Discard the pork bones.

6. Whisk in the shoyu, mirin, salt, ginger, and chili oil (if using).

7. Use this broth immediately or let cool and refrigerate for up to 3 days or freeze for up to 1 month.

SESAME MISO BROTH

SKILL LEVEL: Moderate • **PREP TIME:** 10 minutes • **COOK TIME:** 30 minutes • **YIELD:** Makes 2 quarts (1.9 L)

TO MAKE IN ADVANCE

Basic Dashi (page 28)

INGREDIENTS

1 cup (144 g) white sesame seeds
2 tablespoons (30 ml) sesame oil
2 large garlic cloves, minced
**1 piece (1½ inches, or 3.5 cm) fresh
   ginger, peeled and finely grated**
**2 quarts (1.9 L) Basic Dashi (or dashi
   made with an instant mix)**
½ cup (120 ml) sake (rice wine)
½ cup (136 g) shiro (white) miso
½ cup (136 g) aka (red) miso
Roasted chili oil, to taste (optional)

HOT TIP

If you use a coffee grinder,
be careful not to overprocess
the seeds or you'll end up with
sesame paste. Stop grinding
before the seeds start to
release oil or the powder
will clump.

If you are in a rush, this recipe can be made with dashi from a powder or liquid concentrate and with already ground and toasted sesame seeds. I use both white and red miso here because white miso has a sweeter taste and red miso is stronger, which balances the broth. If you like it spicy, I suggest starting with a very small amount of chili oil and adding more according to your taste preference.

INSTRUCTIONS

1. In a small skillet over low heat, toast the sesame seeds for about 10 minutes, until fragrant and golden brown, constantly stirring or swirling the seeds in the pan as they cook. Let cool, then transfer to a mortar with a pestle or clean coffee grinder. Crush the toasted sesame seeds into a fine powder (see Hot Tip).

2. In a 4-quart (3.8 L) hot pot or large saucepan over medium-high heat (about 425°F, or 220°C, in an electric hot pot), heat the sesame oil until shimmering.

3. Add the garlic and ginger. Cook for about 1 minute until fragrant.

4. Stir in the dashi, sake, white and red miso pastes, and ground sesame seeds. Add the chili oil if you like it spicy. Bring the mixture to a boil, reduce the heat to low, and simmer for 10 minutes. If the broth evaporates too much while cooking and becomes thick, add more dashi; if you do not have any dashi on hand, water is also fine.

5. This broth can be made ahead and refrigerated for up to 3 days or frozen for up to 1 month.

TONYU (SOY MILK) BROTH

SKILL LEVEL: Easy • **PREP TIME:** 10 minutes • **COOK TIME:** 30 minutes • **YIELD:** Makes 2 quarts (1.9 L)

TO MAKE IN ADVANCE

Basic Dashi (page 28)
Chicken Stock (page 30)

INGREDIENTS

3 cups (720 ml) unsweetened soy milk

2 cups (480 ml) Basic Dashi (or dashi made with an instant mix)

2 cups (480 ml) Chicken Stock (or store-bought low-sodium chicken broth)

½ cup (136 g) shiro (white) miso

½ cup (120 ml) sake (rice wine)

¼ cup (60 ml) shoyu (Japanese soy sauce)

½ teaspoon chili oil (optional)

1 tablespoon (15 ml) red pepper flakes (optional)

This simple broth is heartwarming and creamy, but miraculously dairy-free because it contains soy milk. It pairs well with both proteins and vegetables and goes well with almost any dipping sauce. I've made the spicy chili oil and the red pepper flakes optional, but they add a nice kick that complements the silky soy milk base. Try this broth in my Ground Chicken Tonyu (Soy Milk) Nabe (page 85) for something more similar to a stew or my Yasainabe with Tonyu (page 124) for a shabu-shabu–style hot pot brimming with veggies.

INSTRUCTIONS

1. Heat a 4-quart (3.8 L) hot pot or large saucepan over medium-high heat (about 425°F, or 220°C, in an electric hot pot).

2. Add the soy milk, dashi, chicken stock, miso, sake, and shoyu. Bring to a boil, whisking occasionally, until everything is incorporated. If you like it spicy, add the chili oil and red pepper flakes.

3. Cover, reduce the heat to low, and simmer for 20 minutes to let the flavors develop.

4. This broth can be made ahead and refrigerated for up to 3 days or frozen for up to 1 month.

CREAMY CORN BROTH

SKILL LEVEL: Moderate • **PREP TIME:** 20 minutes • **COOK TIME:** 35 minutes • **YIELD:** Makes 2 quarts (1.9 L)

TO MAKE IN ADVANCE

Chicken Stock (page 30)

INGREDIENTS

2 tablespoons (28 g) unsalted butter

1 medium Vidalia onion, chopped

3 cups (463 g) raw corn kernels (from about 4 cobs; or frozen corn kernels, thawed)

1 teaspoon freshly grated nutmeg

3 cups (700 ml) Chicken Stock (or store-bought low-sodium chicken broth)

2 cups (475 ml) whole milk

1 cup (240 ml) heavy cream

¼ cup (68 g) shiro (white) miso

1 teaspoon kosher salt

¼ teaspoon freshly ground black pepper

This broth gets its silky texture and subtle sweetness from fresh corn, and its creaminess from the whole milk and heavy cream. It is best made when corn is at its peak, but you can make it year-round with frozen corn. I also like this hot pot because it's not too heavy. The chicken stock thins it out a bit and gives it the perfect consistency for hot pot cooking. This broth is not ideal for making ahead and freezing because of the dairy, but it cooks in about 30 minutes and is still easy to pull together on a weeknight.

INSTRUCTIONS

1. In a 4-quart (3.8 L) hot pot or large saucepan over medium-high heat (about 425°F, or 220°C, in an electric hot pot), melt the butter. Add the onion. Cook for about 10 minutes, stirring occasionally, until translucent.

2. Add the corn and nutmeg. Cook for about 10 minutes, until the corn is just tender.

3. Stir in the remaining ingredients and bring to a boil. Cover the pot, reduce the heat to low, and simmer until the corn is tender and the broth is very flavorful, about 10 minutes.

4. Scrape the broth into a blender and puree it until smooth or use an immersion blender right in the pot.

5. Use this broth for a hot pot or sip on its own.

JAPANESE CURRY BROTH

SKILL LEVEL: Moderate • **PREP TIME:** 20 minutes • **COOK TIME:** 1 hour • **YIELD:** Makes 2 quarts (1.9 L)

TO MAKE IN ADVANCE
Chicken Stock (page30)

INGREDIENTS

1 tablespoon (15 ml) olive oil
2 large garlic cloves, minced
1 piece (1 inch, or 2.5 cm) fresh ginger, peeled and finely grated
1 medium sweet onion, thinly sliced
¼ cup (½ stick, or 56 g) unsalted butter
¼ cup (30 g) all-purpose flour
2 tablespoons (30 ml) curry powder
1 tablespoon (15 ml) garam masala
¼ teaspoon instant espresso powder (not ground; needs to be powder)
¼ teaspoon ground white pepper
¼ cup (60 ml) shoyu (Japanese soy sauce)
¼ cup (60 g) packed dark brown sugar
2 tablespoons (32 g) tomato paste
5 cups (1.2 L) Chicken Stock (or store-bought low-sodium chicken broth)

Like most Japanese, I grew up eating Japanese curry out of a box with roux cubes you added to hot water. Although I have fond memories of those curried stews, I wanted to try it from scratch with freshly toasted spices and aromatics, such as garlic and ginger. Japanese curries are different from other curries because they are less spicy and have a subtle sweetness that kids tend to like (my kid-friendly Beef Curry Nabe on page 42 will please even the pickiest kids).

This broth gets its rich color and depth from caramelized onion and a toasty roux that has a touch of bitter espresso powder mixed in. A roux is a combination of fat and flour (in this case, we use butter) used to thicken broth. The coffee flavor is very subtle, but it goes well with fattier cuts of meat such as beef. I use dark brown sugar because it gives a darker color and richer flavor to the broth than regular brown sugar. Traditional Japanese curry is much thicker than the consistency of this broth, but I've made it intentionally thinner so you can use it as a hot pot base.

INSTRUCTIONS

1. In a 4-quart (3.8 L) hot pot or large saucepan over medium-high heat (about 425°F, or 220°C, in an electric hot pot), heat the olive oil. Add the garlic and ginger. Cook for about 2 minutes, stirring occasionally, until fragrant.

2. Add the onion. Reduce the heat to medium. Cook for about 20 minutes, stirring and scraping up any brown bits from the bottom of the pot, until the onion starts to caramelize. Using a slotted spoon, transfer the onion and aromatics to a small bowl. Set aside.

3. In the same pot over medium heat, melt the butter. Add the flour. Cook for about 5 minutes, stirring constantly with a wooden spoon, until the roux is pale brown and smells nutty.

4. Stir in the curry powder, garam masala, espresso, and white pepper. Continue to cook until fragrant and a deep brown, about 2 minutes.

5. Return the onion and aromatics to the pot. Stir in the shoyu, brown sugar, tomato paste, and chicken stock. Bring the broth to a boil.

6. Cover the pot, reduce the heat to low, and simmer for about 20 minutes, until the broth is thickened slightly and is very flavorful.

7. This broth can be made ahead and refrigerated for up to 1 week or frozen for up to 2 months.

TOMATO BROTH

SKILL LEVEL: Moderate • **PREP TIME:** 20 minutes • **COOK TIME:** 30 minutes • **YIELD:** Makes 2 quarts (1.9 L)

TO MAKE IN ADVANCE

Vegetable Stock (page 31)

INGREDIENTS

1 tablespoon (15 ml) vegetable oil

1 medium red bell pepper, finely chopped

½ medium sweet onion, finely chopped

2 celery ribs, finely chopped

1 medium carrot, finely grated

2 large garlic cloves, finely grated

½ teaspoon ground fennel seeds

½ teaspoon ground cinnamon

½ teaspoon ground cumin

1 teaspoon kosher salt

½ teaspoon freshly ground black pepper

1 teaspoon fresh lemon thyme (or fresh regular thyme)

2 bay leaves

2 cans (8 ounces, or 227 g, each) tomato sauce

6 cups (1.4 L) Vegetable Stock (or store-bought low-sodium vegetable broth)

½ teaspoon roasted chili oil, plus more as needed (optional)

I like this broth because it holds its own even without being incorporated into a hot pot—the aromatics of the fennel, cinnamon, and cumin really deepen the flavor of the tomato and make this a comforting dish on a cold winter's day. Finely chopping all the vegetables will fill every spoonful with added texture and flavor. If you have a food processor, make your life easier and just throw them all in there in big chunks and pulse away.

INSTRUCTIONS

1. In a 4-quart (3.8 L) hot pot or large saucepan over medium-high heat (about 425°F, or 220°C, in an electric hot pot), heat the vegetable oil. Add the red bell pepper, onion, celery, carrot, and garlic. Cook for about 10 minutes, stirring, until softened and the onion is translucent.

2. Stir in the fennel seeds, cinnamon, cumin, salt, and pepper. Cook for 2 minutes.

3. Add the thyme, bay leaves, tomato sauce, and vegetable stock. Bring the mixture to a boil. If you like it spicy, stir in the chili oil with red pepper flakes.

4. Cover the pot, reduce the heat to low, and simmer for about 10 minutes, until very flavorful. Remove and discard the bay leaves before using as your hot pot base.

5. This broth can be made ahead and refrigerated for up to 3 days or frozen for up to 1 month.

THAI COCONUT CURRY BROTH

SKILL LEVEL: Moderate • **PREP TIME:** 20 minutes • **COOK TIME:** 30 minutes • **YIELD:** Makes 2 quarts (1.9 L)

TO MAKE IN ADVANCE

Chicken Stock (page 30)
Vegetable Stock (page 31)

INGREDIENTS

1 tablespoon (15 ml) vegetable oil
2 tablespoons (32 g) red curry paste
3¼ cups (780 ml) full-fat coconut
    milk
1 quart (960 ml) Chicken Stock or
    Vegetable Stock (or store-bought
    low-sodium chicken broth or
    vegetable broth)
¼ cup (48 g) lychee (about 6 small,
    canned lychee), finely chopped
¼ cup (40 g) finely chopped
    pineapple
1½ tablespoons (23 ml) fish sauce
1 tablespoon (9 g) grated palm sugar,
    or (15 g) light brown sugar
4 kaffir lime leaves
1 teaspoon kosher salt

This soup has many layers: the creamy coconut milk soothes the complex curry paste, the brininess from the fish sauce gives it all the salt you need, and the pineapple and lychee make it slightly sweet and sour. From poultry to seafood, this soup base is very versatile, plus it is gluten-free, low-carb, and paleo. With the option to make it vegetarian by swapping out vegetable stock for the chicken, it can please anyone. For this reason, I like to make it ahead and keep it refrigerated for quick, flavorful meals. On a busy weeknight, I serve it poured over a hot bowl of steamed rice, finished with a mess of fresh herbs on top. If you're looking for something with a little more heartiness, try the rich and savory Thai Chicken Coconut Curry Hot Pot (page 79) or get your mushroom fill with my Magic Mushroom Hot Pot (page 122).

INSTRUCTIONS

1. In a 4-quart (3.8 L) hot pot or large saucepan over medium-high heat (about 425°F, or 220°C, in an electric hot pot), heat the vegetable oil. Add the curry paste. Cook for about 2 minutes, stirring, until fragrant.

2. Stir in the coconut milk, chicken stock, lychee, pineapple, fish sauce, sugar, lime leaves, and salt. Bring to a boil.

3. Cover the pot, reduce the heat to low, and simmer for about 20 minutes, until very flavorful.

4. This broth can be made ahead and refrigerated for up to 3 days or frozen for up to 1 month.

MONGOLIAN BROTH

SKILL LEVEL: Advanced • **PREP TIME:** 20 minutes • **COOK TIME:** 20 minutes • **YIELD:** Makes 2 quarts (1.9 L)

TO MAKE IN ADVANCE

Chicken Bone Broth (page 34)

INGREDIENTS

Original

9 cups (2 L) Chicken Bone Broth (or store-bought chicken bone broth)

20 garlic cloves, peeled and crushed

2 negi (Japanese green onions; or 4 large scallions), coarsely chopped

1 piece (5 inches, or 13 cm) fresh ginger, peeled and thinly sliced

10 whole cloves

6 dried jujubes (red dates)

6 star anise

4 black cardamom pods

4 dried bay leaves

4 dried astragalus root slices (¼ ounce, or 7 g)

¼ cup (8 g) dried lotus seeds

2 tablespoons (13 g) dried goji berries

1½ teaspoons kosher salt

1 teaspoon cumin seeds

¼ teaspoon ground white pepper

Spicy (see Hot Tip)

12 Chinese dried red chile peppers, halved

1 teaspoon Chinese chili powder (or red pepper flakes)

Chili oil, to taste

This deeply aromatic, luxurious broth was inspired by the well-known Mongolian hot pot chain, Little Sheep Hot Pot. Try my Mongolian Lamb Hot Pot (page 131) that incorporates both the original and the spicy versions of this broth. Unlike Japanese hot pots, Mongolian broth is laden with different aromatics and spices, such as black cardamom pods and dried goji berries, that make it so rich and savory, you'll want to save it for a cold day and sip it down all on its own. The skill level on this recipe is advanced because, although the techniques are fairly simple, many of the ingredients can be difficult to find. While most can be purchased at Asian specialty food markets or online, it does require extra time for sourcing (however, it's worth the effort!). The bone broth is what gives it an unctuous texture, so it's best not to substitute regular broth.

INSTRUCTIONS

1. Heat a hot pot or large saucepan over medium-high heat (about 425°F, or 220°C, in an electric pot). If making both broths, heat a split hot pot or 2 medium saucepans over medium-high heat.

2. **To make the Original broth:** Add all the ingredients to the pot. If making both broths, divide the ingredients equally between the 2 pots.

3. **To make the Spicy broth:** Add the chiles, chili powder, and chili oil to one pot.

4. Increase the heat to high and bring the broth(s) to a boil.

5. Cover the pot(s), reduce the heat to low, and simmer for about 10 minutes, until fragrant and very flavorful. Do not strain the aromatics from the broth.

6. This broth can be made ahead and refrigerated for up to 3 days or frozen for up to 1 month.

HOT TIP

The ingredient amounts for the Spicy broth are for a half batch, as you will be splitting the Original recipe between 2 pots. If you want to make a full batch of Spicy broth, double the Spicy ingredients.

VIETNAMESE BROTH

SKILL LEVEL: Moderate • **PREP TIME:** 20 minutes • **COOK TIME:** 30 minutes • **YIELD:** Makes 2 quarts (1.9 L)

TO MAKE IN ADVANCE
Chicken Stock (page 30)

INGREDIENTS
1 tablespoon (15 ml) vegetable oil

1 small Vidalia onion, thinly sliced

1 large tomato, cut into ½-inch-thick (13 mm) wedges

3 quarts (2.8 L) Chicken Stock (or store-bought low-sodium chicken broth)

5 kaffir lime leaves

3 lemongrass stalks, tough outer layers removed, cut into 4-inch (10 cm) pieces, and crushed

½ cup (80 g) finely chopped pineapple

¼ cup (64 g) tom yum paste (see Hot Tip)

1 tablespoon (9 g) grated palm sugar, or (15 g) light brown sugar

1 teaspoon fish sauce

HOT TIP

Tom yum paste is typically made from lemongrass, shallots, garlic, kaffir lime leaves, galangal, lime juice, fish sauce, red pepper flakes, and soybean oil. There are multiple varieties, so look for one rich in color and made in Thailand. You can find it at Asian markets and online.

Every two weeks I go to this amazing Vietnamese eyelash technician, named Alice, who works out of her house. Every time I go, I walk in the door and find myself drifting toward the mouthwatering smells wafting from her kitchen. The air is filled with scents of star anise, fish sauce, fresh basil, and lemongrass—it's her adorable mother who's always cooking away in the kitchen. I asked her how she makes her Vietnamese hot pot broth, and she told me it's very simple: chicken stock, tomatoes, lemongrass, and fish sauce. She inspired me to make this hot and sour broth with spicy tom yum paste and flecks of sweet pineapple (another tip I learned from her). Try it with my Spicy Vietnamese Oxtail Hot Pot (page 113). The tempting aroma is sure to draw curious guests to your kitchen too.

INSTRUCTIONS

1. In a 4-quart (3.8 L) hot pot or large saucepan over medium-high heat (about 425°F, or 220°C, in an electric pot), heat the vegetable oil. Add the onion and tomato. Cook for about 5 minutes, stirring, until the onion is translucent and the tomato is softened.

2. Add the chicken stock, lime leaves, lemongrass, pineapple, tom yum paste, sugar, and fish sauce. Increase the heat to high and bring to a boil.

3. Cover the pot, reduce the heat to low, and simmer for about 20 minutes, until aromatic and very flavorful. Do not strain the aromatics from the broth.

4. This broth can be made ahead and refrigerated for up to 3 days. Gently reheat on the stovetop.

KOREAN KIMCHI BROTH

SKILL LEVEL: Easy • **PREP TIME:** 20 minutes • **COOK TIME:** 40 minutes • **YIELD:** Makes 2 quarts (1.9 L)

TO MAKE IN ADVANCE
Vegetable Stock (page 31)

INGREDIENTS
1 tablespoon (15 ml) vegetable oil

3 to 5 dried chile peppers of your choice, halved with seeds (depending on your heat preference)

½ medium sweet onion, thinly sliced

10 cups (2.4 L) Vegetable Stock (or store-bought low-sodium vegetable broth; substitute anchovy stock if available and you're not concerned with having a vegetarian broth)

1 pound (454 g) kimchi with juices

6 tablespoons (90 ml) distilled white vinegar

3 tablespoons (38 g) sugar

2 tablespoons (32 g) gochujang (Korean red chile paste)

2 tablespoons (34 g) aka (red) miso

2 tablespoons (30 ml) mirin (sweet rice wine)

1 tablespoon (15 ml) sesame oil

1 tablespoon (15 ml) shoyu (Japanese soy sauce)

Kimchi is a traditional Korean condiment of vegetables—typically cabbage—fermented with ingredients such as fish sauce, garlic, *gochugaru* (Korean chile pepper), ginger, and salt. It has a layered, spicy kick that gives this broth its complexity. Also, the great part about kimchi is you can often find really good premade, organic (and local!) brands at your grocery store. When choosing, look for vibrant color, freshness of vegetables, and no additives, like MSG. Kimchi tends to have a lot of zest, so I've added mirin and miso as my Japanese twist to give it some sweet and savory flavors. This broth is vegetarian, so you can use it as a base for any vegetarian hot pot. Or, if you enjoy meat, try my delicious Korean Short Ribs with Spicy Kimchi Nabe (page 110) using this broth.

INSTRUCTIONS

1. In a 4-quart (3.8 L) hot pot or large saucepan over medium-high heat (about 425°F, or 220°C, in an electric hot pot), heat the vegetable oil. Add the dried chiles. Cook for about 1 minute, stirring, until fragrant. Add the onion. Cook for about 5 minutes, stirring, until translucent.

2. Stir in the vegetable stock, kimchi and its juices, vinegar, sugar, gochujang, miso, mirin, sesame oil, and shoyu. Increase the heat to high and bring the broth to a boil.

3. Cover the pot, reduce the heat to low, and simmer for about 30 minutes, until fragrant and very flavorful.

4. This broth can be made ahead and refrigerated for up to 3 days or frozen for up to 1 month.

MACANESE BROTH

SKILL LEVEL: Moderate • **PREP TIME:** 10 minutes • **COOK TIME:** 3 hours 30 minutes • **YIELD:** Makes 2 quarts (1.9 L)

INGREDIENTS

5 pounds (2.3 kg) pork bones, rinsed (see Hot Tips)

1 piece (1 inch, or 2.5 cm) fresh ginger, peeled and finely grated

10 dried jujubes (red dates)

2 tablespoons (13 g) dried goji berries

Kosher salt, to taste

Ground white pepper, to taste (see Hot Tips)

This broth was created by my friend and chef Emily Lai. Among her many other culinary projects, Emily is currently running a Malaysian pop-up in San Francisco called masak | masak. Characteristic of Macanese cooking, each dish is rich and multilayered with spices and aromatics—and this broth is no exception. The jujubes and goji berries provide a subtle sweetness and lend a fresh, floral note. Bonus: now that you have these ingredients on hand, you can use them in my Mongolian Lamb Hot Pot (page 131) as well. Or try this hot pot base simmered with your choice of shabu-shabu–style sliced meat and ingredients like mung bean noodles and yuba (tofu skin) in Emily's Meat Lover's Macanese Hot Pot (page 134).

HOT TIPS

Ask your butcher for pork knuckles, trotters, leg, neck, or hipbones. Almost any bones will work with this recipe.

Start with minimal amounts of salt and pepper and add more to taste. White pepper is strong and has a very distinct flavor.

INSTRUCTIONS

1. In a large stockpot over high heat, combine the pork bones with enough water to cover, approximately 1 gallon (3.8 L). Bring to a boil. Cook for 15 minutes. Remove the bones and rinse them thoroughly to remove any scum. Discard the water and wipe out the stockpot.

2. In the same stockpot over high heat, just cover the cleaned pork bones with fresh water. Add the ginger, jujubes, and goji berries. Bring to a boil.

3. Reduce the heat to low and simmer the broth for about 3 hours, uncovered, until very flavorful and aromatic. Strain the broth into a clean pot and season with salt and pepper. Discard the bones and aromatics.

4. Use this broth immediately or let cool and refrigerate for up to 1 week or freeze for up to 2 months.

PONZU SAUCE

SKILL LEVEL: Easy • **PREP TIME:** 10 minutes • **YIELD:** Makes 1½ cups (360 ml)

INGREDIENTS

- ¾ cup (180 ml) shoyu (Japanese soy sauce)
- 6 tablespoons (90 ml) mirin (sweet rice wine)
- ¼ cup (60 ml) yuzu juice (from 2 fresh yuzu or bottled; or the juice of 1 lemon and 1 lime)
- 2 tablespoons (12 g) peeled, grated daikon radish
- 2 scallions, white part only, thinly sliced

The delicate citrus flavor of a yuzu is what makes this sauce so addictive (trust me; you'll want to put it on everything). Bottled yuzu can be found at Asian markets, but if you're lucky enough to find the fruit fresh, this is the place to use it. Yuzu is a difficult flavor to replicate, but if you can't find yuzu juice, a combination of fresh lemon and lime juices comes pretty close. I like a ponzu sauce that is more *shoyu* (Japanese soy sauce) heavy, versus being too acidic, so I use a very high-quality, strong-tasting soy sauce here. Ponzu sauce is great with anything, but I prefer it with hot pots containing meat or seafood.

INSTRUCTIONS

1. In a small bowl, whisk together all the ingredients until blended.

2. This sauce can be refrigerated for up to 1 week.

SWEET-AND-SOUR LAYU CHILI SAUCE

SKILL LEVEL: Easy • **PREP TIME:** 5 minutes • **YIELD:** Makes ¾ cup (180 ml)

INGREDIENTS

¼ cup (60 ml) shoyu (Japanese soy sauce)

¼ cup (60 ml) mirin (sweet rice wine)

2 tablespoons (30 ml) rice wine vinegar

1 tablespoon (16 g) hoisin sauce

2 teaspoons Sriracha

5 or 6 dashes layu (or chili oil), plus more to taste

I originally created this sauce as an accompaniment to my Spicy Vietnamese Oxtail Hot Pot (page 113), because so many Vietnamese dishes play with that hot, sweet-and-sour balance. My secret ingredient here is *layu*, a Chinese chili oil commonly used as a Japanese condiment to add spice to any dish. The mirin and hoisin sauce give this sauce its sweetness, the vinegar gives it that little bit of sour tang, and the layu and sriracha come in for a sneaky kick at the end. If you're a fiend for heat and are serving this with a mild dish, feel free to amp up the spice with more sriracha and layu.

INSTRUCTIONS

1. In a small bowl, whisk together all the ingredients until smooth.

2. This sauce can be made ahead and refrigerated for up to 1 week.

CHIRIZU SAUCE

SKILL LEVEL: Easy • **PREP TIME:** 10 minutes • **YIELD:** Makes ¾ cup (180 ml)

INGREDIENTS

¼ cup (60 ml) yuzu juice (from 2 fresh yuzu or bottled; or the juice of 1 lemon and 1 lime)

¼ cup (60 ml) sake (rice wine)

3 tablespoons (45 ml) shoyu (Japanese soy sauce)

1 tablespoon (15 ml) mirin (sweet rice wine)

2 tablespoons (20 g) finely grated onion

1 piece (1 inch, or 2.5 cm) fresh ginger, peeled and finely grated

1 tablespoon (6 g) finely grated daikon radish

¼ teaspoon shichimi togarashi (or red pepper flakes)

Yuzu, a sour citrus fruit used prominently in Japanese cooking, is the star of this bright, punchy sauce. You can buy good bottled yuzu juice, but if you're lucky enough to find the tangerine-size fruit fresh, take advantage of it. This sauce is similar to a traditional Ponzu Sauce (page 60), but grated radish and ginger, plus the shichimi togarashi, are added for a peppery kick. It's great for finishing fish because it adds a pleasant hit of acidity, which goes nicely with lean proteins. Serve a little bit in small bowls alongside your hot pot, as fish and vegetables only need a quick dip.

INSTRUCTIONS

1. In a small bowl, stir together all the ingredients until blended.

2. This sauce can be made ahead and refrigerated for up to 1 week.

CHILI-CILANTRO-LIME SAUCE

SKILL LEVEL: Easy • **PREP TIME:** 5 minutes • **YIELD:** Makes ½ cup (120 ml)

INGREDIENTS

½ cup (8 g) loosely packed fresh
    cilantro leaves
¼ cup (60 g) sambal oelek
¼ cup (60 ml) water
2 tablespoons (30 ml) fresh lime
    juice (from 1 lime)
Kosher salt, to taste

This is one of my friend Emily Lai's favorite sauces and her inspiration comes from Hainan, a small province in the southernmost part of China. It's typically served with Hainanese poached chicken rice, one of the region's most traditional and popular dishes. She told me there is a Thai version of this dish called Khao Man Gai, and in Vietnam, it's called Com Ga Hai Nam. She suggests that this sauce goes well with everything because it has the right balance of spice, tartness, and sweetness, along with herbaceous notes.

Emily has even given a recipe for Hainanese poached chicken rice if you want to try to make it: "Poach a whole chicken in a water broth of ginger, cilantro, and scallions, low and slow. Shock the cooked chicken in ice water. Slice or cut the chicken. Make rice with the poaching liquid. Serve the rice and chicken with the broth and two sauces. It's definitely a skill to make this, although it sounds simple. It's one of my favorite things to eat!"

INSTRUCTIONS

1. In a food processor, combine the cilantro, sambal oelek, water, and lime juice. Puree until smooth.

2. Season with salt.

3. This sauce can be made ahead and refrigerated for up to 2 days.

SESAME MISO SAUCE

SKILL LEVEL: Easy • **PREP TIME:** 10 minutes • **COOK TIME:** 10 minutes • **YIELD:** Makes 1½ cups (360 ml)

INGREDIENTS

½ cup (72 g) white sesame seeds
½ cup (136 g) shiro (white) miso
2 tablespoons (30 ml) sugar
1 tablespoon (15 ml) shoyu
    (Japanese soy sauce)
1 tablespoon (15 ml) mirin (sweet
    rice wine)
2 teaspoons rice vinegar
2 large garlic cloves, crushed
¾ cup (180 ml) water, plus more if
    needed
1 tablespoon (15 ml) toasted
    sesame oil

The key to this rich, nutty sauce is to toast the sesame seeds beforehand. Pre-toasted sesame seeds are fine in a pinch, but I suggest toasting them a little further to enhance the flavor. The final swirl of sesame oil also amps up the bold sesame flavor. I like to keep a jar of this sauce in the refrigerator because you can serve it with almost anything—as a sauce for meats and vegetables fresh out of the hot pot, as a salad dressing, or as a dip for crudités.

INSTRUCTIONS

1. In a small skillet over low heat, toast the sesame seeds for about 10 minutes, until fragrant and golden brown, constantly stirring or swirling the seeds in the pan as they cook. Let cool, then transfer to a mortar with a pestle or clean coffee grinder. Crush the toasted sesame seeds into a fine powder (See Hot Tip).

2. In a blender, combine the miso, sugar, shoyu, mirin, vinegar, garlic, water, and the ground sesame seeds. Puree until smooth. The sauce should have the consistency of a salad dressing. Add more water, if needed.

3. Scrape the sauce into a small bowl and stir in the sesame oil before serving.

4. This sauce can be made ahead and refrigerated for up to 1 week.

HOT TIP

If you use a coffee grinder, be careful not to overprocess the seeds or you'll end up with sesame paste. Stop grinding before the seeds start to release oil or the powder will clump.

STEAMED JAPANESE RICE (GOHAN)

SKILL LEVEL: Easy • **PREP TIME:** 10 minutes • **COOK TIME:** 1 hour 15 minutes • **YIELD:** 4 to 6 servings

INGREDIENTS

2 cups (400 g) white or brown Japanese short-grain rice

HOT TIP

You may find my method for cooking rice in this recipe a bit unusual, but I promise it works—every time. We don't measure the cooking water with a cup, we measure it with our thumb. Regardless of how much rice you use or whether or not you cook your rice in a saucepan or rice cooker, this trick works!

Japanese rice is a shorter grain that is higher in starch than long-grain rice, which gives it that signature sticky consistency. It comes in brown varieties, too, and there is also a delicious in-between rice called haiga. When looking at the different types, the higher quality rice you purchase, the better it will taste. If you are at an Asian or a Japanese market, you'll see a range of rices to choose from, so try a few different brands to find your favorite.

INSTRUCTIONS

1. Place the rice in a fine-mesh sieve. Gently rinse the rice with cold water and rub the grains together in your palms to loosen the starches, releasing the milky water. Repeat 4 to 6 times until the water runs clear.

2. Add the rice to a 4-quart (3.8 L) saucepan or 4- to 6-cup (960 ml to 1.4 L) rice cooker and pat it down into an even layer. Cover the rice with enough water so when the tip of your thumb touches the surface of the rice, the water rises to your knuckle—about 1 inch (2.5 cm). Let the rice soak in the water for about 15 minutes. (This makes for a fluffier final product, especially if your rice is not super fresh and a tad dried out.)

3. If using a rice cooker, follow the manufacturer's instructions. If using a saucepan, place the washed rice and clean water over high heat and bring to a boil.

4. Reduce the heat to low, cover the pan, and simmer until just tender, about 30 minutes for white rice and about 40 minutes for brown rice.

5. Remove the saucepan from the heat and let the rice steam, covered, for about 15 minutes. Fluff with a fork and serve.

ROASTED NORI (SEAWEED)

SKILL LEVEL: Easy • **PREP TIME:** 2 minutes • **COOK TIME:** 5 minutes • **YIELD:** Makes about 40 small roasted seaweed squares

INGREDIENTS

10 sheets nori (seaweed), approximately 8 x 8 inches (20 x 20 cm)

Cooking spray, preferably sesame or coconut oil

Fine sea salt, for sprinkling

These days you can find roasted and flavored seaweed in grocery stores, coffee shops—even vending machines. While I appreciate the convenience of pre-roasted nori, I prefer to roast my own because I feel like some of the varieties out there are too oily or don't stay crisp. If you purchase a package of big sheets of unroasted seaweed for sushi, you can roast them over an open gas flame in seconds, which results in much fresher, crispier, and toastier sheets. Plus, you can make many more for the cost. I promise you'll never go back to those instant packs. My kids like to snack on these plain, as if they are potato chips, but they can also be rolled up with rice, slipped into a bowl of ramen, or wrapped up like sushi hand rolls with fresh fish and julienned vegetables. One thing to note, you do need a gas range to make these!

INSTRUCTIONS

1. Line a plate with paper towels and set aside.

2. Spray both sides of each seaweed sheet with cooking spray or use a paper towel to apply a thin coat of oil on each side.

3. Over a low flame on a gas stovetop, using tongs, gently waft the seaweed back and forth on both sides until it crisps up, about 5 seconds. Be careful not to hold the seaweed directly over the flame for too long or it will catch fire. Transfer the roasted seaweed to the prepared plate and sprinkle with salt. Repeat with the remaining seaweed.

4. Transfer the toasted nori to a cutting board and lay 5 sheets on top of each other. Using a chef's knife or kitchen shears, cut the stack into 4 small squares. Repeat with the remaining 5 sheets of roasted nori.

5. Store in an airtight container or resealable plastic bag for up to 3 days.

PORK HOT POTS

KUROBUTA PORK NABE MILLE-FEUILLE

SKILL LEVEL: Easy • **PREP TIME:** 15 minutes • **COOK TIME:** 45 minutes • **YIELD:** 6 to 8 servings •
PREPARATION: Stovetop

TO MAKE IN ADVANCE

Vegetable Stock (page 31)
Sesame Miso Sauce (page 63)
Steamed Japanese Rice (page 64)

INGREDIENTS

¼ cup (68 g) shiro (white) miso
¼ cup (60 g) tahini
¼ cup (60 ml) sake (rice wine) or
    white wine
6 cups (1.4 L) Vegetable Stock
    (or store-bought low-sodium
    vegetable broth)
1 piece (2 inches, or 5 cm) fresh
    ginger, peeled and finely grated
4 teaspoons (20 ml) shoyu
    (Japanese soy sauce)
2 cups (475 ml) water
2 pounds (907 g) thinly sliced (about
    ¼ inch, or 6 mm, thick) pork belly,
    preferably Kurobuta
1 head Napa cabbage, cleaned,
    trimmed, and leaves separated
Sesame Miso Sauce, for dipping
Steamed Japanese Rice, for serving

One of the most beautiful dishes from my friend Emily Lai, this nabe mille-feuille is a savory Japanese take on the classic French dessert made with thin layers of puff pastry. The layering of the cabbage and pork emulates this French dish, which translates to "thousand leaves." It's a visually appealing dish that is very popular in Japan. It is simple yet well seasoned because of the fatty pork, Kurobuta, which comes from a Berkshire pig, is highly marbled, and tends to have darker and more flavorful meat. If you can't find Kurobuta pork, use any other type of heritage-breed pork to give it that juicy tenderness.

INSTRUCTIONS

1. In a large saucepan over medium-high heat, combine the miso, tahini, sake, vegetable stock, ginger, shoyu, and water. Whisk to combine. Bring the mixture to a boil. Reduce the heat to low and simmer while you assemble the hot pot, about 15 minutes.

2. Sandwich 1 slice of pork between 2 cabbage leaves. Cut crosswise into three 2- to 3-inch (5 to 7.5 cm) sections and set aside on a work surface.

3. In a 4-quart (3.8 L) hot pot or large saucepan, nestle the cabbage and pork on their sides, cut sides up, in the pot—they should fit snugly. Repeat with the remaining cabbage and pork until all the pork is used up. If you have remaining cabbage leaves, tuck them in around the edges of the pot and anywhere there is a gap.

4. Heat the hot pot over medium-high heat (about 425°F, or 220°C, in an electric hot pot) until you can hear the pork and cabbage begin to sizzle, 3 to 4 minutes.

5. Pour the warm broth over the cabbage and pork until just covered, and bring to a boil. Cover the pot and reduce the heat to low. Simmer for about 20 minutes, until the cabbage is tender and the pork is cooked through.

6. Serve in shallow bowls with some broth poured over the top, along with the sesame miso sauce for dipping and steamed rice on the side.

PORK SUKIYAKI

SKILL LEVEL: Moderate • **PREP TIME:** 20 minutes • **COOK TIME:** 15 minutes • **YIELD:** 4 to 6 servings •
PREPARATION: Tableside

TO MAKE IN ADVANCE
Basic Sukiyaki Sauce (page 37)

INGREDIENTS

1 pound (454 g) pork loin, very thinly sliced (see Hot Tip)

6 ounces (170 g) Chinese green beans (or regular green beans), trimmed and cut diagonally into 2-inch (5 cm) pieces

5 ounces (140 g) king trumpet mushrooms (or brown cremini mushrooms), cleaned, trimmed, and sliced lengthwise

3 baby bok choy, quartered lengthwise

1 small purple daikon radish (or ½ medium white daikon radish), peeled and thinly sliced

1 pound (454 g) prepared white shirataki noodles, drained and divided into 3-ounce (85 g) portions

4 rectangular pieces of aburaage (fried tofu), sliced

2 tablespoons (30 ml) bacon fat (or sesame oil), divided

1 medium shallot, thinly sliced, divided

½ cup (120 ml) Basic Sukiyaki Sauce, divided

Black sesame seeds, for garnishing

HOT TIP

Freeze the pork up to 4 hours so it is firm and easier to slice or purchase sukiyaki or shabu-shabu pork at Asian markets or ask your butcher to thinly slice it.

Sukiyaki is probably my favorite type of nabe because you can use the Basic Sukiyaki Sauce (page 37) with any meat and vegetable combination. You can even make it vegetarian and increase the amounts of tofu and vegetables. Eat the finished sukiyaki with a bowl of rice or add noodles directly to the hot pot to soak up all the umami-rich sauce. I'm a big fan of the combination of pork and veggies in this recipe: the crisp green beans and daikon radish go well with a tender, saucy piece of pork.

INSTRUCTIONS

1. Arrange the pork, vegetables (except the shallot), noodles, and tofu on platters. Place the platters on the table around the hot pot.

2. In a 4-quart (3.8 L) hot pot or large saucepan over medium-high heat (about 425°F, or 220°C, in an electric hot pot), heat 1 tablespoon (15 ml) of the bacon fat. Add half the shallot. Cook for 2 minutes, stirring, until translucent.

3. Add half the vegetables and noodles to the pot. Cook for about 2 minutes, stirring occasionally, until the vegetables begin to soften.

4. Arrange half the sliced pork on top of the vegetables. Drizzle with ¼ cup (60 ml) of the sukiyaki sauce.

5. Reduce the heat to medium. Cook for about 1 minute, until the pork begins to turn white. Flip the pork and cook for 1 minute more.

6. Fold the cooked pork into the vegetables and noodles until evenly coated with the sauce. Cook until the pork and vegetables are just tender, about 1 minute more. If food starts to stick to the bottom of the hot pot, reduce the heat and add a little water to cool it down.

7. Transfer the pork sukiyaki to plates. Garnish with black sesame seeds and serve.

8. Repeat the process with the remaining 1 tablespoon (15 ml) bacon fat and shallot, followed by the remaining vegetables, noodles, tofu, pork, and ¼ cup (60 ml) sukiyaki sauce.

PORK BELLY TONKOTSU
(PORK BONE BROTH) NABE

SKILL LEVEL: Moderate • **PREP TIME:** 20 minutes, plus 1 hour soaking time • **COOK TIME:** 20 minutes •
YIELD: 4 to 6 servings • **PREPARATION:** Tableside

TO MAKE IN ADVANCE

Pork Bone (Tonkotsu) Broth
(page 38)
Sweet-and-Sour Layu Chili Sauce
(page 61)
Steamed Japanese Rice (page 64)

INGREDIENTS

½ head radicchio, cut into 1-inch
(2.5 cm) wedges
1 pound (454 g) pork belly, very
thinly sliced (see Hot Tip)
½ large lotus root, peeled and sliced
¼ inch (6 mm) thick
3 medium carrots, julienned
3 ounces (85 g) buna-shimeji or
enoki mushrooms, cleaned and
trimmed
1 cup (128 g) Korean rice ovaletts
18 ounces (509 g) prepared udon
noodles, drained
2 quarts (1.9 L) Pork Bone (Tonkotsu)
Broth
Sweet-and-Sour Layu Chili Sauce,
for dipping
Steamed Japanese Rice, for serving

This lusciously creamy hot pot is the most soothing dinner on a cold winter night. Here, I use a silky Tonkotsu Broth (page 38) as the base and serve tender, thinly sliced pork belly alongside it for guests to swish in the hot soup. Nothing compares to juicy, tender pork belly—it adds so much flavor to the broth. If you're able to make this broth over the weekend and buy presliced pork belly at the Asian market, this soup is easily doable on a weeknight for the family.

Another specialty ingredient that truly makes this hot pot shine is the Korean rice ovaletts. They are small, chewy dumpling-like disks made from rice flour and often used in stir-fries and soups. These little cakes have the ideal texture for soaking up whatever flavorful liquid you put them in, making them perfect for hot pots.

INSTRUCTIONS

1. In a large bowl filled with ice water, soak the radicchio for 1 hour to get rid of its bitterness. Drain well.

2. Arrange the pork belly, vegetables, ovaletts, and noodles on platters. Place the platters on the table around the hot pot.

3. Heat a 4-quart (3.8 L) hot pot or large saucepan over medium-high heat (about 425°F, or 220°C, in an electric pot). Add the tonkotsu broth and bring to a boil.

4. Let guests add their own pork belly, vegetables, and ovaletts to the hot broth, swishing back and forth until tender and cooked through, 1 to 2 minutes. As food is added, adjust the heat to maintain a low boil. Serve with the layu chili sauce for dipping and steamed rice on the side.

5. When all the pork and vegetables have been eaten, add the udon noodles to the broth. Cook for 2 to 3 minutes, stirring, until heated through. Serve the noodles as the shime (end-of-meal course).

HOT TIP

Freeze the pork up to 4 hours so it is firm and easier to slice or purchase sukiyaki or shabu-shabu pork at Asian markets or ask your butcher to thinly slice it.

PORK WONTONS
WITH MACANESE BROTH HOT POT

SKILL LEVEL: Moderate • **PREP TIME:** 20 minutes • **COOK TIME:** 20 minutes • **YIELD:** 6 servings •
PREPARATION: Stovetop

TO MAKE IN ADVANCE

Macanese Broth (page 58)
Mom's Pork Wontons (page 148)

INGREDIENTS

1 tablespoon (15 ml) vegetable oil
½ medium Vidalia onion, thinly sliced
2 black garlic cloves (or regular
    garlic), chopped (see Hot Tips)
2 quarts (1.9 L) Macanese Broth (see
    Hot Tips)
24 Mom's Pork Wontons
3 baby bok choy, quartered
    lengthwise
3 ounces (85 g) enoki mushrooms,
    cleaned and trimmed
1 sweet potato, peeled and shredded
    (or 6 ounces, 170 g, spiralized
    sweet potato)
2 large scallions, white and light
    green parts only, cut diagonally
    into 2-inch (5 cm) lengths
1 block (14 ounces, or 395 g) firm
    tofu, drained and cut into 1-inch
    (2.5 cm) cubes

If you live in Colorado, like I do, you know the weather will always be a topic of conversation. One day it's bright and sunny and you want to wear flip-flops, and the next day you're bundling up with a beanie on and it's snowing. It was one of the last snowy days in late spring when I made this hot pot for my family. We passed the time inside by making wontons together, and I told them how I used to make them with my family for our church fair when I was growing up. They always enjoy eating and trying new things when they participate in the cooking, so they loved this hot pot—the wontons almost fill with the broth like a soup dumpling and cook fairly quickly because of the small amount of filling in them. My kids gobbled up their four wontons pretty fast, but feel free to add more if you know you've got little wonton lovers like I do!

INSTRUCTIONS

1. In a 4-quart (3.8 L) hot pot or large saucepan over medium-high heat (about 425°F, or 220°C, in an electric pot), heat the vegetable oil. Add the onion. Cook for 4 to 5 minutes, stirring, until translucent. Add the black garlic. Cook for about 1 minute, until fragrant.

2. Add the Macanese broth and bring the mixture to a boil.

3. Add the wontons. Reduce the heat to low, cover the pot, and simmer for 5 minutes.

4. Add the vegetables and tofu. Cover the pot and cook for 5 minutes more, until the wontons are cooked through and the vegetables are tender.

5. Ladle into shallow bowls and serve.

HOT TIPS

Black garlic is fermented garlic that is sweet and savory, with a deep molasses-like flavor and a soft consistency. You can find it in specialty food shops and online.

This recipe is easy to scale up or down. Just make sure your hot pot is filled about halfway with broth. If the liquid reduces over time, add more.

PORK GOMA (GROUND SESAME) MISO NABE

SKILL LEVEL: Moderate • **PREP TIME:** 30 minutes • **COOK TIME:** 30 minutes • **YIELD:** 4 to 6 servings • **PREPARATION:** Tableside

TO MAKE IN ADVANCE

Basic Dashi (page 28)

INGREDIENTS

8 ounces (227 g) pork loin, very thinly sliced (see Hot Tip)

2 cups (100 g) bean sprouts

4 ounces (113 g) shiitake mushrooms, cleaned and stemmed

¼ head Napa cabbage, cored and thick white parts cut into bite-size pieces

1 bunch shungiku (chrysanthemum leaves; or watercress), stemmed

1 large carrot, thinly sliced on the diagonal

1 pound (454 g) fresh ramen noodles

5 teaspoons (14 g) white sesame seeds

1 tablespoon (15 ml) vegetable oil

8 ounces (227 g) ground pork

½ teaspoon garlic powder

2 quarts (1.9 L) Basic Dashi (or dashi made with an instant mix)

4 teaspoons (23 g) aka (red) miso

4 teaspoons (20 g) neri goma (Japanese sesame paste; or tahini)

2 teaspoons shoyu (Japanese soy sauce)

1 teaspoon sugar

My brother-in-law Victor told me that I had to meet his neighbor Kiko Asaoka. He said I would be amazed by her knowledge of Japanese cooking. I learned she had travelled the world extensively as a diplomat's wife and often entertained and cooked for guests. This recipe, along with others throughout the book that Kiko has shared with me, are an extension of her devotion to preserving the freshness and natural quality of an ingredient without it being over-spiced. For the toasty, nutty sesame flavor in this pork nabe, Kiko uses both ground and roasted white sesame seeds and a sesame paste. The paste, called *neri goma*, uses seeds that are roasted much longer than those used to make tahini, resulting in a richer, more savory flavor that pairs perfectly with pork; however, if you can't find it, use tahini.

INSTRUCTIONS

1. Arrange the sliced pork, vegetables, and noodles on platters. Place the platters on the table around the hot pot.

2. In a medium skillet over low heat, toast the sesame seeds for about 10 minutes, stirring, until fragrant and golden brown. Transfer to a mortar with a pestle or a clean coffee grinder and crush the toasted seeds into a fine powder. Wipe out the skillet.

3. In a 4-quart (3.8 L) hot pot or large saucepan over medium-high heat (about 425°F, or 220°C, in an electric pot), heat the vegetable oil. Add the ground pork and garlic powder. Cook for about 10 minutes, breaking up the meat with a spoon, until cooked through.

Freeze the pork up to 4 hours so it is firm and easier to slice or purchase sukiyaki or shabu-shabu pork at Asian markets or ask your butcher to thinly slice it.

4. Stir in the dashi, miso, neri goma, shoyu, sugar, and ground toasted sesame seeds. Bring to a boil, stirring occasionally. Reduce the heat to low. Simmer for about 5 minutes, until the miso, sesame paste, and sugar dissolve.

5. Let guests add their own sliced pork and vegetables, swishing back and forth in the hot broth until tender and cooked through, 1 to 2 minutes. As food is added, adjust the heat to maintain a low boil.

6. After the meat and vegetables have been eaten, add the ramen noodles to the broth. Cook for 2 to 3 minutes, stirring, until heated through. Serve the noodles as a shime (end-of-meal course).

CHICKEN HOT POTS

THAI CHICKEN COCONUT CURRY HOT POT

SKILL LEVEL: Moderate • **PREP TIME:** 20 minutes • **COOK TIME:** 30 minutes • **YIELD:** 6 to 8 servings • **PREPARATION:** Stovetop

TO MAKE IN ADVANCE

Thai Coconut Curry Broth (page 50)
Steamed Japanese Rice (page 64)

INGREDIENTS

3 pounds (1.3 kg) boneless, skinless chicken thighs, cut into bite-size pieces
Kosher salt, to taste
Freshly ground black pepper, to taste
2 tablespoons (30 ml) vegetable oil, divided
2 quarts (1.9 L) Thai Coconut Curry Broth (see Hot Tip)
6 baby eggplants (such as Thai or fairy tale), stemmed and quartered (or 1 medium eggplant, cut into bite-size pieces)
½ small kabocha (Japanese pumpkin), seeded and thinly sliced
¼ head Napa cabbage, cored and thick white parts cut into bite-size pieces
1 cup (150 g) cherry tomatoes
2 cups (70 g) loosely packed fresh Thai or regular basil leaves
¼ cup (72 g) stemmed, seeded, and minced bird's-eye chiles (or Fresno chiles; optional)
Steamed Japanese Rice, for serving

The most difficult thing about this recipe was coming up with a name for it. My Thai friend, Katie, explained to me that you cannot call a curry a hot pot in Thailand because they are two separate things. Thai curries are traditionally thicker in consistency, while Thai hot pots are more similar to traditional dashi-based Japanese recipes. I think the creaminess of the coconut milk and the robust profile of curry lend themselves well to hot pots—the meat and vegetables soak up so much of that flavor in a brief time. Here, I use a base that has all the complexity of a creamy Thai curry, but it is thinned out with a bit of chicken broth for swishing your vegetables in.

INSTRUCTIONS

1. Season the chicken with salt and pepper.

2. In a large skillet over medium-high heat, heat 1 tablespoon (15 ml) of the vegetable oil. Add half the chicken. Cook for 4 to 5 minutes, stirring once or twice, until browned, but not cooked through. Transfer to a clean bowl and repeat with the remaining 1 tablespoon (15 ml) oil and chicken.

3. Heat a 4-quart (3.8 L) hot pot or large saucepan over medium-high heat (about 425°F, or 220°C, in an electric hot pot). Add the broth and chicken, and bring to a boil. Reduce the heat to medium-low and simmer for 5 minutes.

4. Add the eggplants, kabocha, cabbage, and tomatoes. Continue simmering for about 5 minutes more, until the vegetables are tender and the chicken is cooked through. Stir in the basil and chiles (if using).

5. Ladle into shallow bowls and serve with the steamed rice on the side.

HOT TIP

This recipe is easy to scale up or down. Just make sure your hot pot is filled about halfway with broth. If the liquid reduces over time, add more.

CHICKEN SUKIYAKI

SKILL LEVEL: Moderate • **PREP TIME:** 15 minutes • **COOK TIME:** 15 minutes • **YIELD:** 4 to 6 servings • **PREPARATION:** Tableside

TO MAKE IN ADVANCE
Basic Sukiyaki Sauce (page 37)
Sesame Miso Sauce (page 63)

INGREDIENTS

1 pound (454 g) chicken breasts, very thinly sliced (see Hot Tip)

5 ounces (140 g) wood ear or shiitake mushrooms, cleaned

3 baby bok choy, quartered lengthwise

1 bunch shungiku (chrysanthemum leaves) or watercress, stemmed

1 large carrot, shaved into thin ribbons with a vegetable peeler

½ medium sweet onion, thinly sliced

½ small satsuma imo (Japanese sweet potato) or regular sweet potato, peeled and very thinly sliced on a mandoline

1 block (14 ounces, or 395 g) firm tofu, drained and cut into 1-inch (2.5 cm) cubes

18 ounces (509 g) prepared white shirataki noodles, drained and divided into 3-ounce (85 g) portions

2 tablespoons (30 ml) vegetable oil, divided

2 large garlic cloves, minced, divided

½ cup (120 ml) Basic Sukiyaki Sauce, divided, plus more as needed

Toasted sesame seeds, for garnishing

Sesame Miso Sauce, for serving

Another family favorite, this sukiyaki came about when my in-laws were visiting, and I wanted to show them how to make it. They were huge fans of the easy preparation and liked trying new vegetables they had never heard of; however, you don't need to worry if you can't get your hands on those specialty ingredients. Almost any leftover vegetable in your fridge will work here. Broccoli? Yes! Sliced bell peppers? Totally. My in-laws also could not get enough of the creamy, nutty Sesame Miso Sauce (page 63). The savory sauce is perfect for dunking the tender, delicately seasoned chicken and vegetables. This hot pot is not super filling, so the shirataki noodles cooked in the remaining sukiyaki sauce perfectly round out the meal. But if you are protein lovers, add more chicken. In-law success!

INSTRUCTIONS

1. Arrange the chicken, vegetables, tofu, and noodles on platters. Place the platters on the table around the hot pot.

2. In a 4-quart (3.8 L) hot pot or large saucepan over medium-high heat (about 425°F, or 220°C, in an electric hot pot), heat 1 tablespoon (15 ml) of the vegetable oil until shimmering. Add half the garlic. Cook for about 1 minute, stirring, until fragrant.

3. Add half the vegetables and tofu to the pot. Cook for about 2 minutes, stirring occasionally, until the vegetables begin to soften.

4. Arrange half the sliced chicken on top of the vegetables and drizzle with ¼ cup (60 ml) of the sukiyaki sauce. Reduce the heat to medium. Cook for about 1 minute, until the chicken begins to turn white. Flip the chicken and cook for 1 minute more.

5. Fold the chicken into the vegetables and tofu until evenly coated with the sauce. Continue to cook until the chicken is cooked through and the vegetables are just tender, about 1 minute more. If food starts to stick to the bottom of the hot pot, reduce the heat and add a little water to cool it down.

6. Transfer the chicken sukiyaki to plates and garnish with sesame seeds. Serve with the sesame miso sauce.

7. Repeat the process with the remaining 1 tablespoon (15 ml) vegetable oil, garlic clove, vegetables, tofu, chicken, and ¼ cup (60 ml) sukiyaki sauce.

8. When the vegetables, tofu, and chicken have been eaten and you are left with just the sauce in the bottom of the hot pot, add the shirataki noodles. Cook for 2 to 3 minutes, stirring, until heated through and coated with the sauce, adding more sauce, if needed. Serve the noodles as the shime (end-of-meal course).

CHANKO NABE (SUMO WRESTLER HOT POT)

SKILL LEVEL: Moderate • **PREP TIME:** 40 minutes • **COOK TIME:** 20 minutes, plus 1 hour soaking time • **YIELD:** 4 to 6 servings • **PREPARATION:** Stovetop

TO MAKE IN ADVANCE

Basic Dashi (page 28)
Steamed Japanese Rice (page 64)

INGREDIENTS

Meatballs

½ cup (64 g) cornstarch
1 pound (454 g) ground chicken (dark meat only)
2 scallions, white and light green parts only, thinly sliced
2 dried shiitake mushrooms, soaked in warm water for 1 hour, drained, and finely chopped
½ medium Vidalia onion, finely chopped
1 piece (1 inch, or 2.5 cm) fresh ginger, peeled and finely grated
1 teaspoon sake (rice wine)
1 teaspoon sugar
1 teaspoon kosher salt
⅛ teaspoon freshly ground black pepper

Nabe

2 quarts (1.9 L) Basic Dashi (or dashi made with an instant mix)
½ cup (120 ml) shoyu (Japanese soy sauce)
½ cup (120 ml) sake (rice wine)
1 teaspoon sugar
1 teaspoon kosher salt
8 ounces (227 g) pork loin, very thinly sliced (see Hot Tip)
8 ounces (227 g) large shrimp (6 to 8 shrimp), shelled, tails on, and deveined
1 block (14 ounces, or 395 g) firm silken tofu, drained and cut into 1-inch (2.5 cm) cubes

The name of this hearty nabe recipe from my friend Kiko translates to "parent and child," referring to the close bond between sumo wrestlers and their communal eating habits. Traditionally, this was a dish that teammates would make for each other to help gain weight—it's packed with lean proteins and vegetables that give sumo wrestlers the strength and energy for competing. These days, this is a popular family meal in Japan and one that Kiko grew up eating. The ground chicken meatballs are the best part of this nabe; they are flavored with dried shiitakes, instead of fresh, for added umami and a deeper mushroom flavor. The tender meatballs float in the dashi-based broth like plump dumplings. While you might not be feeding a team of sumo wrestlers, I promise this nabe will be equally successful at satisfying your family and friends.

INSTRUCTIONS

1. **To make the meatballs:** Bring a large pot of water to a boil over high heat. Line a plate with paper towels and set aside. Spread the cornstarch in a shallow bowl.

2. In a large bowl, mix together all the remaining meatball ingredients. (Be careful not to overmix or the meatballs will be dense.) Wet your hands with a little water and form the mixture into Ping-Pong–size balls. You should have about 12 meatballs. Dredge the meatballs in the cornstarch and transfer to a plate.

3. Gently drop the meatballs into the boiling water and cook until they rise to the surface and are partially cooked through, about 2 minutes. Using a slotted spoon, transfer the parboiled meatballs to the paper towel–lined plate to drain.

4. **To make the nabe:** Heat a 4-quart (3.8 L) hot pot or large saucepan over medium-high heat (about 425°F, or 220°C, in an electric pot). Add the dashi, shoyu, sake, sugar, and salt. Bring to a boil.

1 pound (454 g) prepared white shirataki noodles, drained and divided into 3-ounce (85 g) portions

6 shiitake mushrooms, cleaned and stemmed

5 ounces (140 g) forest nameko mushrooms (or buna-shimeji or enoki mushrooms), cleaned, trimmed, and torn into large pieces

4 large scallions, white and light green parts only, cut diagonally into 3-inch (7.5 cm) lengths

1 medium sweet onion, cut into ¼-inch (0.6 cm)-thick rings

¼ head Napa cabbage, cored and thick white parts cut into bite-size pieces

Steamed Japanese Rice, for serving

HOT TIP

Freeze the pork up to 4 hours so it is firm and easier to slice or purchase sukiyaki or shabu-shabu pork at Asian markets or ask your butcher to thinly slice it.

5. Add the sliced pork, shrimp, tofu, noodles, vegetables, and parboiled meatballs. Cover the pot and reduce the heat to low. Simmer for about 5 minutes, until the pork, shrimp, and meatballs are just cooked through and the vegetables are tender.

6. Ladle into shallow bowls and serve.

7. After the meat, tofu, noodles, and vegetables have been eaten, add the steamed rice to the remaining broth and let it soak up the liquid, like a risotto, stirring occasionally, until most of the broth has been absorbed. Serve the porridge as a shime (end-of-meal course).

SHIO KOJI CHICKEN WITH VEGETABLES NABE (TORI NO MIZUTAKE)

SKILL LEVEL: Moderate • **PREP TIME:** 30 minutes, plus 2 hours marinating time • **COOK TIME:** 30 minutes • **YIELD:** 4 to 6 servings • **PREPARATION:** Stovetop

TO MAKE IN ADVANCE

Chicken Stock (page 30)
Steamed Japanese Rice (page 64)

INGREDIENTS

1½ pounds (680 g) boneless skinless chicken thighs, cut into bite-size pieces

4 ounces (113 g) shiitake mushrooms, cleaned and stemmed

Kosher salt, to taste

Freshly ground black pepper, to taste

4 tablespoons (60 g) shio koji, divided

2 tablespoons (30 ml) olive oil, divided

2 tablespoons (30 ml) sesame oil

5 cups (1.2 L) Chicken Stock (or store-bought low-sodium chicken broth)

¼ cup (60 ml) sake (rice wine)

2 tablespoons (30 ml) shoyu (Japanese soy sauce)

2 medium carrots, sliced 1 inch (2.5 cm) thick on the diagonal

2 large scallions, white and light green parts only, cut into 1½-inch (3.5 cm) pieces

1 yellow squash, sliced ¼ inch (6 mm) thick

1 medium red bell pepper, seeded and cut into bite-size pieces

1 bunch shungiku (chrysanthemum leaves) or watercress, stemmed

Steamed Japanese Rice, for serving

This colorful hot pot has a light broth highlighted by the *shio koji*, shoyu, and sake. Shio koji is an umami-rich condiment made from *shio*, or salt, and rice that is fermented with *koji*, the edible fungus used to make miso and sake. By marinating both the chicken and the mushrooms in shio koji, these ingredients then season the broth when added to the hot pot. You can find shio koji at most Japanese markets and online.

INSTRUCTIONS

1. Place the chicken into a medium bowl and the mushrooms into a separate medium bowl. Season each with salt and pepper.

2. Add 3 tablespoons (45 g) of the shio koji to the chicken and the remaining 1 tablespoon (15 g) to the mushrooms. Toss each to coat. Cover each bowl with plastic wrap and refrigerate for 2 hours.

3. In a medium skillet over medium heat, heat 1 tablespoon (15 ml) of the olive oil. Add half the chicken to the skillet. Cook for 4 to 5 minutes, stirring occasionally, until browned, but not fully cooked. Transfer to a clean bowl and repeat with the remaining 1 tablespoon (15 ml) olive oil and chicken. Wipe out the skillet.

4. Return the skillet to medium heat and heat the sesame oil. Add the mushrooms. Cook for 4 to 5 minutes, stirring occasionally, until tender. Transfer to a plate and slice each mushroom in half.

5. Heat a 4-quart (3.8 L) hot pot or large saucepan over medium-high heat (about 425°F, or 220°C, in an electric pot). Add the chicken stock, sake, and shoyu. Bring to a boil.

6. Add the carrots, scallions, squash, red bell pepper, and the chicken and its juices. Cover the pot and reduce the heat to low. Simmer for about 15 minutes, until the vegetables are just tender and the chicken is cooked through. Add the shungiku and mushrooms.

7. Serve in shallow bowls with the steamed rice on the side.

GROUND CHICKEN TONYU
(SOY MILK) NABE

SKILL LEVEL: Easy • **PREP TIME:** 15 minutes • **COOK TIME:** 30 minutes • **YIELD:** 4 to 6 servings •
PREPARATION: Stovetop

TO MAKE IN ADVANCE
Tonyu (Soy Milk) Broth (page 42)
Steamed Japanese Rice (page 64)

INGREDIENTS

1 tablespoon (15 ml) bacon fat (or vegetable oil)

1 piece (1½ inches, or 3.5 cm) fresh ginger, peeled and finely grated

2 large garlic cloves, peeled and minced

1½ pounds (679 g) ground chicken, preferably dark meat

Kosher salt, to taste

Freshly ground black pepper, to taste

5 cups (1.2 L) Tonyu (Soy Milk) Broth

½ small kabocha (Japanese pumpkin), seeded and cut into bite-size pieces

¼ head Napa cabbage, cored and thick white parts cut into bite-size pieces

2 large eggs, lightly beaten

Steamed Japanese Rice, for serving

Shredded nori (seaweed), for garnishing

Shichimi togarashi (or red pepper flakes), to taste, for garnishing

This is one of those Japanese comfort foods perfect for a cold winter's day when you just want to stay in and have something that soothes the soul. The sweetness of the soy milk and miso combine perfectly with the ground chicken and vegetables. Unlike other thick-skinned squash, kabocha does not need to be peeled, so this dish can be pulled together quickly. Also, if you don't have time to make fresh dashi or chicken stock, use store-bought versions.

INSTRUCTIONS

1. In a 4-quart (3.8 L) hot pot or large saucepan over medium-high heat (about 425°F, or 220°C, in an electric hot pot), heat the bacon fat. Add the ginger and garlic. Cook for about 1 minute, stirring, until fragrant.

2. Add the ground chicken. Season with salt and pepper. Cook for about 5 minutes, breaking up the chicken with a spoon, until just cooked through.

3. Add the tonyu broth, increase the heat to high, and bring to a boil.

4. Add the kabocha. Reduce the heat to low, cover the pot, and simmer for about 15 minutes, until the kabocha is just tender.

5. Add the cabbage. Cover the pot and simmer for 5 minutes more.

6. Right before serving, swirl the beaten eggs into the soup. Let stand for 1 minute so the eggs can set.

7. Divide the steamed rice among serving bowls and ladle the soup over the top. Garnish with the nori and sprinkle with shichimi togarashi.

BEEF HOT POTS

KOBE WAGYU BEEF SUKIYAKI

SKILL LEVEL: Easy • **PREP TIME:** 30 minutes • **COOK TIME:** 20 minutes • **YIELD:** 4 to 6 servings • **PREPARATION:** Tableside

TO MAKE IN ADVANCE

Basic Sukiyaki Sauce (page 37)

INGREDIENTS

1½ pounds (680 g) Kobe beef (or rib-eye or Angus beef), very thinly sliced (see Hot Tip)

5 ounces (140 g) shiitake mushrooms, cleaned, trimmed, and sliced

1 bunch watercress, stemmed

1 large carrot, shaved into thin ribbons with a vegetable peeler

1 cup (4 ounces, or 113 g) sugar snap peas, trimmed

1 block (14 ounces, or 395 g) extra-firm silken tofu, drained and cut into 1-inch (2.5 cm) cubes

18 ounces (509 g) prepared udon noodles, drained

2 pieces (1 inch, or 2.5 cm, each) beef suet (or 2 tablespoons, or 30 ml, bacon fat or vegetable oil)

½ medium sweet onion, thinly sliced, divided

½ cup (120 ml) Basic Sukiyaki Sauce, divided, plus more as needed

Toasted white sesame seeds, for garnishing

4 to 6 large eggs, lightly beaten (preferably pasteurized, as they will be eaten raw; optional)

HOT TIP

Freeze the beef up to 4 hours so it is firm and easier to slice. or purchase sukiyaki or shabu-shabu–style beef at Asian markets or ask your butcher to thinly slice it.

I like the ease of this dish—once the Sukiyaki Sauce (page 37) is made, it is an incredibly simple meal you can make with any protein and vegetables you have on hand. Traditional sukiyaki is served with a lightly beaten egg that you dip the cooked beef and vegetables into before eating. This gives the food a silky, luxurious texture that's surprisingly addictive. I recommend serving this with my Simple Salad with Sesame Soy Dressing (page 140).

INSTRUCTIONS

1. Arrange the beef, mushrooms, watercress, carrot, peas, tofu, and noodles on platters. Place the platters on the table around the hot pot.

2. In a 4-quart (3.8 L) hot pot or large saucepan over medium-high heat (about 425°F, or 220°C, in an electric hot pot), melt 1 piece of suet until it is rendered. You may have a bit of cartilage left over, but you can keep it in the pot. Add half the onion. Cook for about 5 minutes, stirring occasionally, until translucent.

3. Add half the vegetables and tofu to the pot. Cook for about 2 minutes, stirring, until the vegetables begin to soften.

4. Arrange half the sliced beef on top of the vegetables. Drizzle with ¼ cup (60 ml) of the sukiyaki sauce. Reduce the heat to medium and cook for about 1 minute, until the beef begins to turn brown. Flip the beef and cook for 1 minute more.

5. Fold the beef into the vegetables and tofu until evenly coated with the sauce. Cook until the beef is tender and almost cooked through, about 1 minute more. If food starts to stick to the bottom of the hot pot, reduce the heat and add a little water to cool it down.

6. Transfer the beef sukiyaki to plates and garnish with sesame seeds. Serve with individual bowls of lightly beaten egg for dipping.

7. Repeat the process with the remaining suet, onion, vegetables, tofu, beef, and ¼ cup (60 ml) sukiyaki sauce.

8. When the vegetables, tofu, and beef have been eaten and you are left with just the sauce in the bottom of the hot pot, add the udon noodles. Cook for 2 to 3 minutes, stirring, until heated through and coated with sauce, adding more sauce, if needed. Serve the noodles as the shime (end-of-meal course).

SLOW-COOKED BEEF BRISKET TOMATO NABE

SKILL LEVEL: Moderate • **PREP TIME:** 20 minutes • **COOK TIME:** 6 hours 30 minutes • **YIELD:** 4 to 6 servings • **PREPARATION:** Stovetop

TO MAKE IN ADVANCE

Tomato Broth (page 49)

INGREDIENTS

2 pounds (907 g) beef brisket

Kosher salt, to taste

Freshly ground black pepper, to taste

1 tablespoon (15 ml) olive oil

2 quarts (1.9 L) Tomato Broth (see Hot Tip)

2 small yellow cauliflower crowns (or other colored variety), cut into bite-size florets

1 bunch shungiku (chrysanthemum leaves; or watercress), stemmed

5 ounces (140 g) king trumpet mushrooms (or brown cremini mushrooms), cleaned, trimmed, and sliced lengthwise

½ small satsuma imo (Japanese sweet potato; or any other variety of sweet potato), thinly sliced

HOT TIP

This recipe is easy to scale up or down. Just make sure your hot pot is filled about halfway with broth. If the liquid reduces over time, add more.

This slow-cooked brisket is an homage to my mother-in-law, Clara, who makes the most tender, flavorful brisket for Passover. Although mine doesn't really compare to hers, my husband says, "It's not half bad,"—so I'll take it. Brisket is perfect for slow cooking because all its connective tissues break down and gelatinize over time. What this means is that, if you are patient, it's one of the juiciest and most succulent cuts of beef you can get. Whatever you do, don't trim off the fat, as that is what traps in the moisture so you aren't left with a dry piece of meat. You can trim off the fat when you slice it later, but I think it's delicious just the way it is. I like to add an extra ladle of broth to everyone's bowls, along with a spoon, so guests can enjoy a nice bowl of soup with meaty bits of goodness at the end.

INSTRUCTIONS

1. Season the brisket with salt and pepper.

2. Heat the olive oil in a large skillet over medium-high heat. Sear the meat in the skillet on all sides until browned, about 6 minutes per side. Transfer to a cutting board.

3. Heat a 4-quart (3.8 L) hot pot or large saucepan over medium-high heat (about 425°F, or 220°C, in an electric pot). Add the tomato broth and bring to a boil.

4. Add the brisket to the broth, fat side down. Cover the pot, reduce the heat to low, and simmer for about 6 hours, until tender and a fork can easily pierce the brisket. Remove the brisket and slice it ¼ inch (6 mm) thick.

5. Add the vegetables and sliced meat to the broth. Simmer for about 10 minutes more, until all the vegetables are tender.

6. Ladle into shallow bowls and serve.

RIB-EYE BEEF SHABU-SHABU

SKILL LEVEL: Moderate • **PREP TIME:** 30 minutes • **COOK TIME:** 15 minutes • **YIELD:** 4 to 6 servings • **PREPARATION:** Tableside

TO MAKE IN ADVANCE

Basic Shabu-Shabu Broth (page 33)
Sesame Miso Sauce (page 63)

INGREDIENTS

1½ pounds (680 g) rib-eye beef, very thinly sliced (see Hot Tips)

8 ounces (about 3 packed cups, or 227 g) butternut squash noodles (or thinly sliced carrots)

6 ounces (170 g) asparagus, trimmed and cut diagonally into 2-inch (5 cm) lengths

3 ounces (85 g) buna-shimeji (brown) mushrooms (or enoki mushrooms), cleaned and trimmed

2 cups (60 g) packed baby spinach

¼ head Napa cabbage, cored and thick white parts cut into bite-size pieces

1 block (14 ounces, or 395 g) firm silken tofu, drained and cut into 1-inch (2.5 cm) cubes

1 pound (454 g) prepared buckwheat soba noodles, drained

2 quarts (1.9 L) Basic Shabu-Shabu Broth (see Hot Tips)

1 leek, white parts only, sliced ¼ inch (6 mm) thick

Sesame Miso Sauce, for serving

The simplicity of shabu-shabu allows the quality of the ingredients to shine through—and this recipe is a classic example of shabu-shabu. It's important to have vegetables that are quick to cook, so make sure your root vegetables are sliced very thinly and keep that in mind if using any substitutes. This is a perfect recipe to make when you can visit a farmers' market and have your pick of what's in season. Splurge on a good rib eye, as the meat is the hero here, and the sesame miso sauce pretty much makes everything better.

INSTRUCTIONS

1. Arrange the beef, vegetables, tofu, and noodles on platters. Place the platters on the table around the hot pot.

2. Heat a 4-quart (3.8 L) hot pot or large saucepan over medium-high heat (about 425°F, or 220°C, in an electric hot pot). Add the shabu-shabu broth and leek and bring to a boil.

3. Let guests add their own meat, vegetables, and tofu, swishing back and forth in the hot broth until the vegetables are tender and the meat is still slightly pink, 1 to 2 minutes. As food is added, adjust the heat to maintain a low boil. Serve with the sesame miso sauce for dipping.

4. After all the meat, vegetables, and tofu have been eaten, add the noodles to the pot. Simmer for 2 to 3 minutes until heated through. Serve the noodles as a shime (end-of-meal course).

HOT TIPS

Freeze the beef up to 4 hours so it is firm and easier to slice or purchase sukiyaki or shabu-shabu beef at Asian markets or ask your butcher to thinly slice it.

This recipe is easy to scale up or down. Just make sure your hot pot is filled about halfway with broth. If the liquid reduces over time, add more.

BEEF CURRY NABE

SKILL LEVEL: Moderate • **PREP TIME:** 20 minutes • **COOK TIME:** 2 hours 15 minutes • **YIELD:** 4 to 6 servings • **PREPARATION:** Stovetop

TO MAKE IN ADVANCE

Japanese Curry Broth (page 46)
Steamed Japanese Rice (page 64)

INGREDIENTS

1½ pounds (680 g) cubed beef stew meat (chuck is best)
Kosher salt, to taste
Freshly ground black pepper, to taste
All-purpose flour, for dusting
1 tablespoon (15 ml) olive oil, plus more as needed
2 quarts (1.9 L) Japanese Curry Broth
12 ounces (340 g) small red potatoes (8 to 10 potatoes), cut into bite-size pieces
4 medium carrots, oblique cut (see Hot Tip)
1 block (14 ounces, or 395 g) extra-firm tofu, drained and cut into 1-inch (2.5 cm) cubes
Steamed Japanese Rice, for serving

Japanese curry is strong in flavor but has a subtle sweetness and isn't terribly spicy, so kids tend to like it over traditional curries. The low-and-slow method of cooking the stew meat in this recipe breaks it down, leaving it juicy and tender—so don't bother getting higher-grade cuts of meat, as it will do the reverse and result in a tough meat when cooked longer. You can add other vegetables, like bean sprouts, Napa cabbage, and shiitake mushrooms, to this hot pot, but to please my kids, I've left only what they like in this one.

INSTRUCTIONS

1. Season the beef with salt and pepper, and dust with flour.

2. In a 4-quart (3.8 L) hot pot or large saucepan over medium-high heat, (about 425°F, or 220°C, in an electric hot pot), heat the olive oil. Add half the beef and cook, turning occasionally, until browned, about 6 minutes. Transfer to a bowl and repeat with more olive oil, if needed, and the remaining beef. Return the cooked beef to the pot.

3. Add the Japanese curry broth and bring to a boil. Reduce the heat to low, cover the pot, and simmer for 1 hour.

4. Add the potatoes and carrots. Cover the pot and cook for 45 minutes more.

5. Add the tofu. Cover and cook until the meat and vegetables are tender and the tofu is heated through, about 15 minutes more.

6. Ladle into shallow bowls and serve with steamed rice.

HOT TIP

To make an oblique cut:
1. Peel the carrots and cut off the stems.

2. Hold each carrot on a cutting surface with your non-dominant hand and hold the knife with your dominant hand at a 45-degree angle.

3. Cutting about 1-inch (2.5 cm) slices on the diagonal, roll the carrot a quarter turn toward you after each cut. Repeat until the carrot is completely cut. The cuts should be angled toward each other.

SHORT RIB SESAME MISO NABE

SKILL LEVEL: Moderate • **PREP TIME:** 20 minutes • **COOK TIME:** 20 minutes • **YIELD:** 4 to 6 servings • **PREPARATION:** Tableside

TO MAKE IN ADVANCE

Sesame Miso Broth (page 41)

Sweet-and-Sour Layu Chili Sauce (page 61)

Steamed Japanese Rice (page 64)

INGREDIENTS

1½ pounds (680 g) boneless beef short ribs, very thinly sliced (see Hot Tips)

8 ounces (227 g) baby red potatoes, thinly sliced

6 small gai lan (Chinese broccoli; or broccolini), trimmed

3 ounces (85 g) ronfun (white) shimeji mushrooms (or enoki mushrooms), cleaned and trimmed

2 cups (about 5 ounces, or 140 g) packed very thinly sliced white cabbage

2 quarts (1.9 L) Sesame Miso Broth (see Hot Tips)

Steamed Japanese Rice, for serving

Sweet-and-Sour Layu Chili Sauce, for dipping

Julienned scallions, for garnishing

The boneless short ribs in this recipe are incredibly tender and soak up the flavor of the sesame miso broth really well. You could get away with no dipping sauce, but the Sweet-and-Sour Layu Chili Sauce (page 61) takes it to another level. Look for well-marbled short ribs for beef that will melt in your mouth.

INSTRUCTIONS

1. Arrange the beef, potatoes, gai lan, mushrooms, and cabbage on platters. Place the platters on the table around the hot pot.

2. Heat a 4-quart (3.8 L) hot pot or large saucepan over medium-high heat (about 425°F, or 220°C, in an electric hot pot). Add the sesame miso broth and bring to a boil.

3. Let guests add their own meat, vegetables, and tofu, swishing back and forth in the hot broth until the vegetables are tender and the meat is still slightly pink, 1 to 2 minutes. As food is added, adjust the heat to maintain a low boil.

4. Serve with the steamed rice on the side and the layu chili sauce for dipping. Garnish with the scallions.

HOT TIPS

Freeze the beef up to 4 hours so it is firm and easier to slice or purchase sukiyaki or shabu-shabu beef at Asian markets or ask your butcher to thinly slice it.

This recipe is easy to scale up or down. Just make sure your hot pot is filled about halfway with broth. If the liquid reduces over time, add more.

SEAFOOD HOT POTS

SEAFOOD MEDLEY SHABU-SHABU

SKILL LEVEL: Moderate • **PREP TIME:** 30 minutes • **COOK TIME:** 15 minutes • **YIELD:** 4 to 6 servings •
PREPARATION: Tableside

TO MAKE IN ADVANCE
Basic Shabu-Shabu Broth (page 33)
Ponzu Sauce (page 60)
Steamed Japanese Rice (page 64)

INGREDIENTS
2 ounces (56 g) dried harusame
    cellophane noodles
Boiling water
1 pound (454 g) large shell-on shrimp
    (12 to 16 shrimp), deveined
1 pound (454 g) littleneck clams,
    scrubbed
6 large sea scallops, rinsed and
    patted dry
8 ounces (227 g) skinless sea bass or
    cod, cut into 2-inch (5 cm) pieces
5 ounces (140 g) eryngii (oyster)
    mushrooms, cleaned, trimmed,
    and torn into small bunches
5 ounces (140 g) forest nameko
    mushrooms (or enoki mushrooms),
    cleaned, trimmed, and torn into
    small bunches
1 leek, white part only, cleaned,
    quartered, and cut into 2-inch
    (5 cm) lengths
4 Napa cabbage leaves, cut into
    bite-size pieces
1 block (14 ounces, or 395 g) firm
    tofu, drained and cut into 1-inch
    (2.5 cm) cubes
2 quarts (1.9 L) Basic Shabu-Shabu
    Broth (see Hot Tip)
1 piece (1½ inches, or 3.5 cm) fresh
    ginger, peeled and thinly sliced
1 tablespoon (15 ml) sesame oil
Steamed Rice, for serving
Ponzu Sauce, for serving

It's important to know that all shabu-shabu starts with a fairly bland broth—it's the ingredients that you gently swish in the broth that add the real flavor. For this seafood-based shabu-shabu, buy the highest-quality fish and shellfish you can find. This dish is a celebration of enjoying food in its simplest and most natural form, so you want every ingredient to be fresh and at its most flavorful. I have accompanied this delicate hot pot with a classic, bright, and citrusy Ponzu Sauce (page 60). When all the seafood and vegetables have been eaten, the remaining broth can be sipped on its own or add rice to make a porridge for the shime (end-of-meal course).

INSTRUCTIONS

1. Place the dried noodles in a large heatproof bowl and cover with the boiling water. Let sit for about 10 minutes, until softened. Rinse under cold water, drain well, and cut in half.

2. Arrange the seafood, vegetables, tofu, and noodles on platters. Place the platters on the table around the hot pot.

3. Heat a 4-quart (3.8 L) hot pot or large saucepan over medium-high heat (about 425°F, or 220°C, in an electric hot pot). Add the shabu-shabu broth, ginger, and sesame oil, and bring to a boil.

4. Let guests add their own seafood, vegetables, tofu, and noodles, swishing back and forth in the hot broth until the noodles and tofu are warm, the vegetables are tender, and the seafood is just cooked, about 6 minutes for the clams, 1 minute for the shrimp and scallops, and about 2 minutes for the fish. If any clams do not open, discard and do not eat them. As food is added, adjust the heat to maintain a low boil.

5. Serve with the steamed rice on the side and the ponzu sauce for dipping.

HOT TIP

This recipe is easy to scale up or down. Just make sure your hot pot is filled about halfway with broth. If the liquid reduces over time, add more.

SALMON HOT POT

SKILL LEVEL: Moderate • **PREP TIME:** 30 minutes • **COOK TIME:** 35 minutes • **YIELD:** 4 to 6 servings •
PREPARATION: Stovetop

TO MAKE IN ADVANCE

Basic Dashi (page 28)
Steamed Japanese Rice (page 64)

INGREDIENTS

1½ pounds (680 g) 1-inch-thick
    (2.5 cm) skin-on salmon fillets
    (preferably Atlantic salmon)
Kosher salt, to taste
Freshly ground black pepper, to taste
1 tablespoon (15 ml) vegetable oil
1 tablespoon (15 ml) sesame oil
½ medium sweet onion, thinly sliced
1 large garlic clove, minced
5 cups (1.2 L) Basic Dashi (or dashi
    made with an instant mix)
2 tablespoons (34 g) shiro (white)
    miso
2 tablespoons (30 ml) sake (rice
    wine)
1½ tablespoons (23 ml) shoyu
    (Japanese soy sauce)
1 tablespoon (15 ml) mirin (sweet
    rice wine)
1 medium carrot, julienned
½ small satsuma imo (Japanese
    sweet potato; or regular sweet
    potato), peeled and very thinly
    sliced on a mandoline
5 ounces (140 g) asparagus, trimmed
    and cut diagonally into 2-inch
    (5 cm) lengths
3 ounces (85 g) enoki mushrooms,
    cleaned, trimmed, and torn into
    bite-size pieces
1 cup (about 4 ounces, or 113 g) bean
    sprouts
1 cup (about 3 ounces, or 85 g)
    loosely packed baby spinach
Steamed Japanese Rice, for serving

My friend Elisabeth Saucier is a fantastic recipe-testing partner; she's a great cook with discerning taste buds and she's not afraid to give me honest feedback. While we were working on this recipe together, Elisabeth had the brilliant idea of gently cooking the salmon separately, and then topping each bowl of steaming soup with the still-pink-inside fish, to poach gently in the broth to tender perfection.

INSTRUCTIONS

1. Season the salmon fillets with salt and pepper. Line a plate with paper towels and set aside.

2. Heat the vegetable oil in a large nonstick skillet over medium-high heat until shimmering. Add the salmon fillets, skin sides down. Cover the skillet and cook for about 5 minutes, until the salmon is opaque on the outside and still a bit raw on the inside. Uncover the skillet and cook for about 1 minute, until the skin gets a little more crispy—this will make it easier to remove the skin. Transfer the salmon to a plate, skin sides up.

3. Using a paring knife, gently remove the skin from the salmon. Return the skin to the skillet and cook over medium-high heat until very crispy on both sides, about 1 minute per side. Transfer the crispy salmon skins to the paper towel–lined plate to drain. Season them with salt. Cut the salmon skins into small strips to use as a topping.

4. In a 4-quart (3.8 L) hot pot or large saucepan over medium-high heat (about 425°F, or 220°C, in an electric hot pot), heat the sesame oil until shimmering. Add the onion. Cook for about 4 minutes, stirring, until lightly browned. Add the garlic. Cook for about 1 minute until fragrant.

5. Add the dashi, miso, sake, shoyu, and mirin, stirring to dissolve the miso. Bring to a boil. Reduce the heat to a simmer. Add the carrot, sweet potato, and asparagus to the pot. Simmer for 5 minutes.

6. Add the mushrooms, bean sprouts, and spinach. Simmer until the vegetables are tender, about 5 minutes more. Cut the salmon into 1-inch-thick (2.5 cm) pieces.

7. Ladle the soup and vegetables into shallow bowls. Top each bowl with 3 or 4 pieces of salmon and garnish with the crispy salmon skin. The salmon will continue to cook in the hot soup. Serve with the steamed rice on the side.

SOFT-SHELL CRAB SPICY MISO NABE

SKILL LEVEL: Moderate • **PREP TIME:** 15 minutes • **COOK TIME:** 30 minutes • **YIELD:** 4 to 6 servings •
PREPARATION: Stovetop

TO MAKE IN ADVANCE
Sesame Miso Broth (page 41)
Ponzu Sauce (page 60)
Steamed Japanese Rice (page 64)

INGREDIENTS
Nonstick cooking spray, preferably
    coconut oil, for greasing
½ cup katakuriko (Japanese potato
    starch; or cornstarch)
12 soft-shell crabs, rinsed (see
    Hot Tips)
5 cups (1.2 L) Sesame Miso Broth
    (see Hot Tips)
2 ears fresh corn, shucked and cut
    into 2-inch (5 cm) pieces
5 ounces (140 g) small shiitake
    mushrooms, cleaned and
    trimmed
1 bunch karashina (Japanese
    mustard cabbage), or arugula
1 large negi (Japanese green onion),
    or 2 scallions, thinly sliced
    lengthwise
1 block (14 ounces, or 395 g) firm
    silken tofu, drained and cut into
    1-inch (2.5 cm) cubes
Steamed Japanese Rice, for serving
Ponzu Sauce, for dipping

HOT TIPS

Soft-shell crabs are usually
sold cleaned, so a light rinse is
all they need.

This recipe is easy to scale
up or down. Just make sure
your hot pot is filled about
halfway with broth. If the liquid
reduces or thickens over time,
add more.

Soft-shell crabs are not traditionally served in hot pots, but I love their subtle brininess and the way the small crab legs puff up and get crispy when fried. Here, I've broiled the soft-shell crabs so they come out crisp without the grease of deep-frying. Just be careful not to let them soak in the soup too long or they lose their crunch. They only need a quick dunk to heat through. Serve with a side of Shio Koji Pickled Vegetables (page 147).

INSTRUCTIONS

1. Preheat the broiler and position a rack in the middle of the oven. Line a rimmed baking sheet with aluminum foil and coat it with cooking spray. Line another baking sheet with paper towels and set aside.

2. Spread the katakuriko in a shallow bowl. Dredge the crabs in the katakuriko until evenly coated; shake off any excess. Transfer the crabs, bottom sides up, to the baking sheet prepared with cooking spray. Make sure they are not touching. Spray the crabs liberally with cooking spray.

3. On the middle rack, broil the crabs for 8 to 10 minutes, or until crispy and golden brown. Watch carefully to make sure they don't burn. Remove the crabs from the oven. Flip them, shell sides up, and broil for 5 to 6 minutes more, or until golden and cooked through. Transfer the crabs to the paper towel–lined baking sheet to drain. Arrange the crabs on a platter and place the platter on the table next to the hot pot.

4. Heat a 4-quart (3.8 L) hot pot or large saucepan over medium-high heat (about 425°F, or 220°C, in an electric hot pot). Add the sesame miso broth and bring to a boil.

5. Add the corn to the broth. Cook, turning if not submerged in the broth, until almost tender, about 8 minutes.

6. Add the remaining vegetables and tofu. Cook for about 2 minutes, until the vegetables are tender and the tofu is heated through. Arrange the soft-shell crabs on top of the vegetables so they can soak up some of the broth but are not fully submerged.

7. Transfer to shallow bowls and serve with the steamed rice on the side and the ponzu sauce for dipping.

TUNA BELLY WITH DASHI NABE

SKILL LEVEL: Moderate • **PREP TIME:** 20 minutes • **COOK TIME:** 10 minutes • **YIELD:** 4 to 6 servings •
PREPARATION: Tableside

TO MAKE IN ADVANCE

Basic Dashi (page 28)
Chirizu Sauce (page 61)
Steamed Japanese Rice (page 64)

INGREDIENTS

1 pound (454 g) quality tuna belly
    (such as ahi), sliced ¼ inch (6 mm)
    thick (see Hot Tips)
5 ounces (140 g) maitake
    mushrooms, trimmed and torn
    into large pieces
3 ounces (85 g) mizuna (Japanese
    mustard greens), stemmed (see
    Hot Tips)
1 large carrot, shaved into thin
    ribbons with a vegetable peeler
½ purple daikon (6 ounces, or 170 g),
    peeled and very thinly sliced on a
    mandoline
¼ head Napa cabbage, cored and
    thick white parts cut into bite-
    size pieces
1 pound (454 g) prepared white
    shirataki noodles, drained and
    divided into 3-ounce (85 g)
    portions
2 quarts (1.9 L) Basic Dashi (or dashi
    made with an instant mix; see Hot
    Tips)
2 large scallions, white and light
    green parts, thinly sliced
2 tablespoons (30 ml) yuzu juice
    (bottled or from 1 fresh yuzu;
    the juice of ½ lemon and ½ lime
    can be substituted)
1 tablespoon (15 ml) shoyu
    (Japanese soy sauce)
1 teaspoon kosher salt
Steamed Japanese Rice, for serving
Chirizu Sauce, for dipping

This hot pot is a perfect midday meal or light dinner because it won't weigh you down with spice or richness. The tuna only needs a few seconds in the dashi—you want it to be tender and raw inside. I also love the Chirizu Sauce (page 61) paired with this hot pot; it's bright and acidic, a natural complement for the tuna without overpowering it.

INSTRUCTIONS

1. Arrange the tuna, vegetables, and noodles on platters. Place the platters on the table around the hot pot.

2. Heat a 4-quart (3.8 L) hot pot or large saucepan over medium-high heat (about 425°F, or 220°C, in an electric hot pot). Add the dashi, scallions, yuzu juice, shoyu, and salt. Bring to a boil.

3. Let guests add their own tuna, vegetables, and noodles, swishing back and forth in the hot broth until the tuna is still slightly raw, just 3 to 5 seconds, and the vegetables and noodles are tender and warmed through, 1 to 2 minutes. As food is added, adjust the heat to maintain a low boil.

4. Serve with the steamed rice on the side and the chirizu sauce for dipping.

HOT TIPS

Refrigerate the tuna up to 4 hours ahead of time so it is firm and easier to slice.

If you cannot find mizuna, use traditional mustard greens. Stem the leaves and cut each leaf into quarters for nice, large pieces.

This recipe is easy to scale up or down. Just make sure your hot pot is filled about halfway with broth. If the liquid reduces over time, add more.

SEAFOOD TOM YUM HOT POT

SKILL LEVEL: Moderate • **PREP TIME:** 30 minutes • **COOK TIME:** 25 minutes • **YIELD:** 6 to 8 servings • **PREPARATION:** Tableside

INGREDIENTS

Broth

2 tablespoons (30 ml) vegetable oil

1 piece (4 inches, or 10 cm) fresh ginger, peeled, sliced, and smashed

1 piece (3 inches, or 7.5 cm) fresh galangal, thinly sliced

6 lemongrass stalks, tough outer layers removed, crushed, and cut into 4-inch (10 cm) pieces

4 garlic cloves, minced

3 shallots, minced

2 quarts (1.9 L) water

¼ cup (64 g) tom yum paste (see Hot Tip)

10 kaffir lime leaves, crushed

4 tomatoes, cut into eighths

2 tablespoons (30 ml) fish sauce

3 bird's-eye chiles (red Thai chiles; optional)

2 tablespoons (30 ml) fresh lime juice (from 1 lime)

Hot Pot

9 ounces (255 g) dried vermicelli noodles

Boiling water

1 pound (454 g) crab, cooked or raw, cut into pieces

8 ounces (227 g) littleneck clams, scrubbed

8 ounces (227 g) mussels, scrubbed and debearded (discard any cracked or open mussels)

8 ounces (227 g) large shell-on shrimp (6 to 8 shrimp)

This fragrant, Thai-inspired recipe from my chef friend Emily Lai incorporates tom yum paste. On its own, the broth has a hot and sour taste, similar to tom yum soup, but the seafood added to the hot pot gives it a sweet brininess with layers of flavor. Here, Emily has given some ideas for the types of seafood and vegetables to use, but consider it a guideline; use what looks freshest or what you have on hand. My suggestion: instead of black cod, you could use monkfish or bass; instead of shiitake, use shimeji, enoki, or maitake mushrooms.

INSTRUCTIONS

1. **To make the broth:** In a 4-quart (3.8 L) hot pot or large saucepan over medium-high heat (about 425°F, or 220°C, in an electric hot pot), heat the vegetable oil. Add the ginger, galangal, and lemongrass. Cook for about 2 minutes, stirring, until fragrant. Add the garlic and shallots. Cook until softened, about 2 minutes more.

2. Add the water, tom yum paste, lime leaves, tomatoes, fish sauce, and chiles (if using). Bring to a boil. Reduce the heat to a simmer and cook for 20 minutes. When ready to eat, increase the heat to medium-high and return the broth to a boil. Stir in the lime juice.

3. **To make the hot pot:** Place the dried vermicelli noodles in a large heat-proof bowl. Cover with the boiling water and let sit for about 10 minutes, until tender and pliable. Rinse under cold water and drain well.

4. Arrange the seafood, fish, vegetables, and noodles on platters. Place the platters on the table around the hot pot.

4 ounces (113 g) calamari legs

8 ounces (227 g) black cod, skin removed and cut into large pieces

3 baby bok choy, quartered lengthwise

4 Napa cabbage leaves, cut into bite-size pieces

4 ounces (113 g) shiitake mushrooms, cleaned and trimmed

Fresh Thai basil leaves, for garnishing

Fresh cilantro leaves, for garnishing

5. Let guests add their own seafood, fish, vegetables, and noodles, swishing back and forth in the hot broth until the noodles are warmed through, the vegetables are tender, and the seafood is just cooked through, about 6 minutes for the crab, clams, and mussels; about 2 minutes for the fish; and about 1 minute for the shrimp and calamari. If any clams or mussels do not open, discard and do not eat them. As food is added, adjust the heat to maintain a low boil.

6. Ladle the soup into shallow bowls, garnish with the basil and cilantro, and serve.

HOT TIP

Tom yum paste is typically made from lemongrass, shallots, garlic, kaffir lime leaves, galangal, lime juice, fish sauce, red pepper flakes, and soybean oil. THere are multiple varieties, so look for one rich in color and made in Thailand. You can find it at Asian markets and online.

SPICY HOT POTS

MUSSELS WITH SPICY TOMATO NABE

SKILL LEVEL: Moderate • **PREP TIME:** 20 minutes • **COOK TIME:** 10 minutes • **YIELD:** 4 to 6 servings •
PREPARATION: Tableside

TO MAKE IN ADVANCE
Tomato Broth, spicy (page 49)

INGREDIENTS

2 quarts (1.9 L) Tomato Broth, spicy
(see Hot Tip)

2 pounds (907 g) mussels, scrubbed
and debearded (discard any
cracked or open mussels)

4 rectangular pieces aburaage (fried
tofu), sliced ¼ inch (6 mm) thick

2 cups (3 ounces, or 85 g) shishito
peppers, stemmed

1 leek, white part only, cleaned, cut
into ¼-inch (6 mm) slices, and
separated

1 yellow squash, stemmed and cut
into ¼-inch (6 mm) slices

1 medium red bell pepper, seeded
and sliced

Juice and zest of 1 lemon

2½ ounces (70 g) daikon radish
sprouts (or bean sprouts)

⅓ cup (3 g) finely chopped fennel
or anise fronds, for garnishing
(optional)

Shichimi togarashi (or red pepper
flakes), for sprinkling

This is a comfort hot pot, perfect for a cold day. I like how the spiciness of this dish comes in all different forms—from the red pepper flakes in the tomato broth to the radish sprouts and shishito peppers. The lemon juice and zest add a fresh but subtle zing that perfectly complements the mussels. The mussels leak a briny liquid gold that seeps into the broth and gives it that salty taste of the sea—similar to a bouillabaisse. I was tempted to break off a crusty French loaf and dip it in the remaining soup, but this dish is hearty enough to eat like a stew and surprisingly filling without any carbs. Fennel isn't for everyone, as it has a very distinct flavor (like licorice), but I think it gives this dish a nice balance with fresh, fragrant herbal notes in every bite. This hot pot comes together very quickly, so don't overestimate how much time the mussels need to cook—the veggies and mussels require only 5 minutes!

INSTRUCTIONS

1. Heat a 4-quart (3.8 L) hot pot or large saucepan over medium-high heat (about 425°F, or 220°C, in an electric pot). Add the spicy tomato broth and bring to a boil.

2. Place the mussels into the broth in the middle of the pot. Surround them with the tofu, followed by the shishito peppers, leek, squash, and red bell pepper. Squeeze the lemon juice over everything and sprinkle with the zest. Cover the pot, reduce the heat to low, and simmer for 5 minutes, until the mussels open. If any mussels do not open, discard and do not eat them.

3. Right before serving, add the radish sprouts. Serve in shallow bowls. Garnish with the fennel (if using) and sprinkle with the shichimi togarashi for extra spice. Leave each guest an extra bowl for the mussel shells.

HOT TIP

This recipe is easy to scale up or down. Just make sure your hot pot is filled about halfway with broth. If the liquid reduces over time, add more.

KOREAN SHORT RIBS WITH SPICY KIMCHI NABE

SKILL LEVEL: Moderate • **PREP TIME:** 40 minutes • **COOK TIME:** 1 hour 10 minutes, plus 30 minutes marinating time • **YIELD:** 4 to 6 servings • **PREPARATION:** Stovetop

TO MAKE IN ADVANCE
Korean Kimchi Broth (page 57)

INGREDIENTS
¼ cup (50 g) sugar

2 pounds (907 g) ½-inch-thick (13 mm) Korean short ribs

1 cup (120 ml) shoyu (Japanese soy sauce)

¼ cup (60 ml) water

2 quarts (1.9 L) Korean Kimchi Broth (see Hot Tip)

3 ounces (85 g) ronfun (white) shimeji mushrooms (or white beech mushrooms), cleaned and trimmed

1 block (14 ounces, or 395 g) firm silken tofu, drained and cut into 1-inch (2.5 cm) pieces

1 cup (about 4 ounces, or 113 g) bean sprouts

18 ounces (509 g) prepared udon noodles, drained

HOT TIP

This recipe is easy to scale up or down. Just make sure your hot pot is filled about halfway with broth. If the liquid reduces over time, add more.

I'll admit, I'm not a huge fan of kimchi on its own because of its strong smell, heavy garlic flavor, and tang—but in this hot pot, the flavors of the kimchi are mellowed by the beef and slow-cooked vegetables, giving a milder yet flavor-packed broth. Also, although it's optional, the crispy Korean Scallion Pancakes (page 153) are the perfect side and add that needed crunch between bites of tender short ribs and stewed vegetables. If you'd like to make this vegetarian, skip the short ribs and add more vegetables and tofu.

INSTRUCTIONS

1. Rub the sugar on the short ribs to coat them thoroughly on both sides.

2. In a medium bowl, stir together the shoyu and water. Coat the short ribs in the mixture and refrigerate for 30 minutes to marinate.

3. Heat a 4-quart (3.8 L) hot pot or large saucepan over medium-high heat (about 425°F, or 220°C, in an electric hot pot). Add the kimchi broth and bring to a boil.

4. Arrange the short ribs around the edge of the hot pot. Cover the pot, reduce the heat to low, and simmer for about 1 hour, until the ribs are fork-tender. Remove the ribs and cut them into thirds so they are easier to plate. Place them back into the hot pot.

5. Add the mushrooms, tofu, and bean sprouts. Cover the pot and simmer for about 5 minutes, until tender.

6. When all the meat and vegetables have been eaten and you are left with just broth, add the udon noodles. Cook for 2 to 3 minutes, or until heated through. Serve the noodles as a shime (end-of-meal course).

SPICY VIETNAMESE OXTAIL HOT POT

SKILL LEVEL: Moderate • **PREP TIME:** 40 minutes • **COOK TIME:** 2 hours 30 minutes to 3 hours •
YIELD: 6 servings • **PREPARATION:** Stovetop

TO MAKE IN ADVANCE

Vietnamese Broth (page 54)
Sweet-and-Sour Layu Chili Sauce (page 61)

INGREDIENTS

1 cup (120 g) all-purpose flour
6 large 2-inch-thick (5 cm) oxtails (about 4 pounds, or 1.8 kg; see Hot Tips)
Kosher salt, to taste
Freshly ground black pepper, to taste
2 tablespoons (30 ml) vegetable oil, plus more as needed
2 quarts (1.9 L) Vietnamese Broth (see Hot Tips)
1 pound (454 g) dried thin rice noodles
Boiling water
Bean sprouts, for garnishing
Fresh Thai basil leaves, for garnishing
Fesh cilantro leaves and tender stems, for garnishing
Thinly sliced jalapeños, for garnishing
Lime wedges, for serving
Sweet-and-Sour Layu Chili Sauce, for dipping

HOT TIPS

Look for high-quality oxtails that have a generous amount of meat surrounding the bone and are on the larger side, so each person will be satisfied with just one.

This recipe is easy to scale up or down. Just make sure your hot pot is filled about halfway with broth. If the liquid reduces over time, add more.

This Vietnamese-style hot pot is one of my all-time favorites. It might appear time-consuming, but this recipe is relatively hands-off while you let the oxtails simmer in the aromatic broth until they're incredibly tender. The slow cooking releases the fat from the bone marrow, giving the hot and sour, tom yum–style broth a silky, unctuous mouthfeel. It's a perfect combination of savory and spicy, with a bright, peppery kick from the fresh herbs and pho-inspired garnishes. The Sweet-and-Sour Layu Chili Sauce (page 61) is also a nod to the classic pho accompaniments hoisin and Sriracha. I like to drizzle a bit of the sauce into my soup to break up the richness, but it's also nice to give everyone a little bowl on the side as a dip for the oxtail meat.

INSTRUCTIONS

1. Spread the flour in a shallow bowl. Season the oxtails with salt and pepper and dredge them in the flour, shaking off any excess.

2. In a 4-quart (3.8 L) hot pot or large saucepan over medium-high heat (about 425°F, or 220°C, in an electric pot), heat the vegetable oil. Add half the oxtails and cook, turning, until browned all over, 5 to 7 minutes. Transfer to a plate and repeat with the remaining oxtails, adding more oil, if needed.

3. Return the oxtails to the hot pot. Add the Vietnamese broth, increase the heat to high, and bring to a boil. Cover the pot, reduce the heat to low, and simmer for 2½ to 3 hours, until the oxtails are tender.

4. Meanwhile, place the dried noodles in a large bowl. Cover the noodles with the boiling water and let sit for 8 to 10 minutes, until tender. Rinse under cold water and drain well.

5. Arrange the sprouts, herbs, jalapeños, and rice noodles on platters. Place the platters on the table around the hot pot.

6. Ladle the soup into bowls, giving each person an oxtail.

7. Let guests add their own bean sprouts, herbs, jalapeño, and noodles. Serve with the lime wedges and the layu chili sauce for dipping.

CRAB LEGS WITH SPICY TONKOTSU
(PORK BONE BROTH) NABE

SKILL LEVEL: Moderate • **PREP TIME:** 20 minutes • **COOK TIME:** 15 minutes • **YIELD:** 4 to 6 servings •
PREPARATION: Tableside

TO MAKE IN ADVANCE

Pork Bone (Tonkotsu) Broth, spicy
(page 38)
Chirizu Sauce (page 61)
Steamed Japanese Rice (page 64)

INGREDIENTS

1½ pounds (680 g) cooked crab legs,
separated
5 ounces (140 g) maitake
mushrooms (or oyster
mushrooms), cleaned, trimmed,
and torn into large pieces
1½ cups (about 2 ounces, or 57 g)
loosely packed stemmed arugula
1½ cups (about 2 ounces, or 57
g) loosely packed fresh baby
spinach
½ large heirloom tomato, cut into
¼-inch-thick (6 mm) wedges
1 block (14 ounces, or 395 g) firm
tofu, drained and cut into 1-inch
(2.5 cm) cubes
12 ounces (340 g) prepared white
shirataki noodles, drained
2 quarts (1.9 L) Pork Bone (Tonkotsu)
Broth, spicy (see Hot Tip)
Finely chopped jalapeño pepper, for
garnishing
Shichimi togarashi (or red pepper
flakes), for garnishing
Steamed Japanese Rice, for serving
Chirizu Sauce, for dipping

This hot pot is not only delicious but a real visual stunner. The coral-hued crab legs, ombre maitake mushrooms, crisp greens, clean white noodles and tofu, and spectrum of reds and greens on an heirloom tomato are a teaser for how bright and complex this dish tastes. I chose to use crab legs versus whole crab because they're easier to crack open, popping out a nice big piece of meat with your chopsticks. I like to serve this with a zesty Chirizu Sauce (page 61); it gives a nice balance to the sweet crab and the spice of the tonkotsu broth.

INSTRUCTIONS

1. Using a chef's knife, cut the crab legs in half crosswise. Then, using kitchen shears, cut a slit along each shell for easier eating. Arrange the crab, vegetables, tofu, and noodles on platters. Place the platters on the table around the hot pot. Provide extra dishes for the discarded crab shells.

2. Heat a 4-quart (3.8 L) hot pot or large saucepan over medium-high heat (about 425°F, or 220°C, in an electric pot). Add the spicy tonkotsu broth and bring to a boil.

3. Let guests add their own crab, vegetables, tofu, and noodles, swishing back and forth in the hot broth until tender and cooked through, 1 to 2 minutes. As food is added, adjust the heat to maintain a low boil. Garnish with the jalapeño and shichimi togarashi, and serve with the steamed rice on the side and the chirizu sauce for dipping.

HOT TIP

This recipe is easy to scale up or down. Just make sure the hot pot is filled about halfway with broth. If the liquid reduces over time, add more.

CHICKEN AND THE EGG NABE

SKILL LEVEL: Moderate • **PREP TIME:** 30 minutes, plus 1 hour marinating time • **COOK TIME:** 20 minutes • **YIELD:** 4 to 6 servings • **PREPARATION:** Stovetop

TO MAKE IN ADVANCE

Sesame Miso Broth, spicy (page 41)
Steamed Japanese Rice (page 64)

INGREDIENTS

Teriyaki Sauce

1 cup (240 ml) shoyu (Japanese soy
    sauce)
1 cup (200 g) sugar
1 piece (1½ inches, or 3.5 cm) fresh
    ginger, peeled and finely grated
2 large garlic cloves, minced
½ cup (120 ml) mirin (sweet rice
    wine)

Nabe

1½ pounds (679 g) boneless skinless
    chicken thighs, cut into bite-size
    pieces
4 cups (960 ml) Sesame Miso Broth,
    spicy
¼ small kabocha (Japanese
    pumpkin), seeded and thinly
    sliced
5 ounces (140 g) king trumpet
    mushrooms (or cremini
    mushrooms), cleaned, trimmed,
    and sliced lengthwise
3 kabu (Japanese turnips; or regular
    turnips), stemmed, peeled, and
    quartered
2 small broccoli crowns, cut into
    bite-size florets
1 large negi (Japanese green onion;
    or 2 scallions), thinly sliced
1 block (14 ounces, or 395 g) yakidofu
    (grilled tofu), drained and cut into
    1-inch (2.5 cm) cubes
4 to 6 large eggs
Steamed Japanese Rice, for serving
Red pepper flakes, for garnishing

This dish reminds me of my childhood when we would eat *oyakodon*, a traditional Japanese comfort food made with chicken and eggs, and laden with a dashi and shoyu–based sauce soaked up by the fluffy steamed rice scooped on top. In this recipe, the combination of the spicy sesame miso broth and marinated chicken teriyaki offers similar flavors to that umami-filled dish my siblings and I craved growing up. This is super kid-friendly, very filling, and one of my family's favorite Sunday night hot pots.

INSTRUCTIONS

1. **To make the teriyaki sauce:** In a medium saucepan over high heat, combine the shoyu, sugar, ginger, and garlic. Bring to a boil. As soon as it boils, reduce the heat to low and whisk in the mirin. Remove from the heat. (Refrigerate the leftover sauce for up to 2 weeks and use as a marinade for salmon, beef, chicken, or vegetables.)

2. **To make the nabe:** In a small bowl, toss the chicken thighs with ¼ cup (60 ml) of the teriyaki sauce. Cover and refrigerate for 1 hour.

3. Heat a 4-quart (3.8 L) hot pot or large saucepan over medium-high heat (about 425°F, or 220°C, in an electric hot pot). Add the spicy sesame miso broth. Bring to a boil.

4. Add the kabocha and chicken to the hot pot. Cover the pot and cook for about 5 minutes, until the kabocha is almost tender.

5. Add the remaining vegetables and tofu. Cook for about 2 minutes, until the vegetables are tender and the tofu is heated through.

6. Crack the eggs into the hot pot, scattered throughout. Cover the pot and cook the eggs until the whites are just set and the yolks are still runny, about 3 minutes—the chicken should be fully cooked at this point.

7. Transfer to shallow bowls and serve with the steamed rice on the side. Garnish with the red pepper flakes.

VEGETABLE HOT POTS

GREEN VEGETABLE NABE

SKILL LEVEL: Easy • **PREP TIME:** 20 minutes • **COOK TIME:** 15 minutes • **YIELD:** 4 to 6 servings • **PREPARATION:** Tableside

TO MAKE IN ADVANCE

Creamy Corn Broth (page 45)
Sesame Miso Sauce (page 63)
Steamed Japanese Rice (page 64)

INGREDIENTS

5 ounces (140 g) asparagus, trimmed and cut diagonally into 2-inch (5 cm) pieces
6 curly kale leaves, stemmed and halved lengthwise
3 baby bok choy, quartered lengthwise
2 small broccoli crowns, cut into bite-size florets
2 quarts (1.9 L) Creamy Corn Broth (see Hot Tip)
Snipped fresh chives, for garnish
Steamed Japanese Rice, for serving
Sesame Miso Sauce, for dipping

This is the perfect hot pot for those times when you need a good dose of heart-healthy green vegetables, but still want something warm and satisfying. It's light enough to serve at lunchtime and comes together quickly as the vegetable preparation is fairly simple. I've chosen green vegetables, such as broccoli and asparagus, that maintain their crisp, natural state even after a few minutes in the sweet and creamy corn broth.

INSTRUCTIONS

1. Arrange the vegetables on a platter. Place the platter on the table around the hot pot.

2. Heat a 4-quart (3.8 L) hot pot or large saucepan over medium-high heat (about 425°F, or 220°C, in an electric hot pot). Add the creamy corn broth and bring to a boil.

3. Let guests add their own vegetables, swishing back and forth for a few minutes in the hot broth until tender and cooked through, 1 to 2 minutes. As food is added, adjust the heat to maintain a low boil.

4. Garnish the cooked vegetables with the chives, and serve with the steamed rice on the side and the sesame miso sauce for dipping.

HOT TIP

This recipe is easy to scale up or down. Just make sure your hot pot is filled about halfway with broth. If the liquid reduces over time, add more.

MAGIC MUSHROOM HOT POT

SKILL LEVEL: Moderate • **PREP TIME:** 20 minutes • **COOK TIME:** 20 minutes • **YIELD:** 4 to 6 servings • **PREPARATION:** Tableside

TO MAKE IN ADVANCE

Thai Coconut Curry Broth (page 50)
Steamed Japanese Rice (page 64)

INGREDIENTS

1 pound (454 g) mixed Japanese mushrooms (such as shiitake, buna-shimeji, enoki, oyster, wood ear, or maitake), cleaned, trimmed, and torn into large pieces

3 Japanese eggplants (or 1 medium eggplant), cut into bite-size pieces

1 small red bell pepper, seeded and thinly sliced

1 small green bell pepper, seeded and thinly sliced

¼ head Napa cabbage, cored and thick white parts cut into bite-size pieces

1 cup (35 g) loosely packed fresh Thai basil leaves (or regular basil leaves), for garnishing

2 quarts (1.9 L) Thai Coconut Curry Broth (see Hot Tip)

Steamed Japanese Rice, for serving

Lime wedges, for serving

This creamy, coconut milk–based hot pot is a great way to experiment with all those types of mushrooms available at your farmers' market or grocery store. It's becoming easier to find Japanese mushrooms beyond shiitake, so don't limit yourself. Swap in whatever edible varieties you find—just pick ones that vary in look and size for a more visually interesting dish. After cooking, don't toss out that leftover broth; the coconut curry is so flavorful on its own, you'll want to spoon some over your rice or sip it straight from the bowl.

INSTRUCTIONS

1. Arrange the vegetables and Thai basil on platters. Place the platters on the table around the hot pot.

2. Heat a 4-quart (3.8 L) hot pot or large saucepan over medium-high heat (about 425°F, or 220°C, in an electric pot). Add the Thai coconut curry broth and bring to a boil.

3. Let guests add their own vegetables, swishing back and forth in the hot broth until tender and cooked through, 1 to 2 minutes. As food is added, adjust the heat to maintain a low boil.

4. Garnish with the Thai basil, and serve with the steamed rice and lime wedges on the side.

HOT TIP

This recipe is easy to scale up or down. Just make sure your hot pot is filled about halfway with broth. If the liquid reduces over time, add more.

VEGETARIAN RICE CONGEE HOT POT

SKILL LEVEL: Moderate • **PREP TIME:** 30 minutes • **COOK TIME:** 40 minutes • **YIELD:** 6 to 8 servings •
PREPARATION: Stovetop

TO MAKE IN ADVANCE
Vegetable Stock (page 31)

INGREDIENTS

Broth

4 garlic cloves, peeled
3 shallots, peeled
2 tablespoons (30 ml) vegetable oil
1 piece (4 inches, or 10 cm) fresh
    ginger, peeled and thinly sliced
6 lemongrass stalks, tough outer
    layers removed, crushed, and cut
    into 4-inch (10 cm) pieces
10 cups (2.4 L) Vegetable Stock
    (or store-bought low-sodium
    vegetable broth)
1½ cups (300 g) short-grain brown
    rice, rinsed well
1½ cups (300 g) short-grain white
    rice, rinsed well
Kosher salt, to taste
Ground white pepper, to taste

Hot Pot

1 block (14 ounces, or 395 g) firm
    silken tofu, drained and cut into
    1-inch (2.5 cm) pieces
4 rectangular pieces aburaage
    (fried tofu), sliced
1 bunch yuba (dried bean curd
    sticks), hydrated for 10 minutes
    in boiling water
¼ head Napa cabbage, cored and
    thick white parts cut into bite-
    size pieces
5 ounces (140 g) enoki mushrooms,
    cleaned, trimmed, and torn into
    small bunches
Soy sauce, for drizzling
Sesame oil, for drizzling
Fried shallots (store-bought is fine),
    for garnishing

My friend Emily Lai has two kids and lots of nieces and nephews, so she's used to making adjustments for kids and making sure her meals are super kid-friendly. She told me that congee is an introductory food for many Asian toddlers, so the textures and flavors in this dish are not foreign to them. Your kids will like the mild flavors of the broth—it's like a warm, filling porridge. Don't forget to wash the rice to remove all the impurities before cooking it, and feel free to improvise and add the veggies your kids or guests prefer!

INSTRUCTIONS

1. **To make the broth:** In a food processor, pulse the garlic and shallots until finely chopped.

2. Heat the vegetable oil in a large skillet over medium-high heat. Add the ginger and lemongrass. Cook for about 2 minutes, until fragrant. Add the chopped garlic and shallots. Cook for about 2 minutes more, until softened.

3. Add the vegetable stock and bring to a boil.

4. Add the brown and white rice. Cover the skillet, reduce the heat to low, and simmer until thickened, stirring occasionally, about 20 minutes. If the congee gets too thick, add ½ cup (120 ml) water. Remove and discard the lemongrass.

5. Using an immersion blender, or in a standard blender and working in batches, puree the congee until it is smooth and has a porridge-like consistency. Season with salt and pepper.

6. **To make the hot pot:** Heat a 4-quart (3.8 L) hot pot or large saucepan over medium-high heat (about 425°F, or 220°C, in an electric hot pot). Add the congee and bring to a boil. Reduce the heat to maintain a simmer.

7. Add the tofu, yuba, cabbage, and mushrooms to the pot. Continue simmering for 10 minutes.

8. Ladle the congee into shallow bowls and drizzle with the soy sauce and sesame oil. Garnish with the fried shallots.

YASAINABE WITH TONYU
(VEGETABLES WITH SOY MILK BROTH)

SKILL LEVEL: Moderate • **PREP TIME:** 20 minutes • **COOK TIME:** 15 minutes • **YIELD:** 4 to 6 servings • **PREPARATION:** Tableside

TO MAKE IN ADVANCE

Tonyu (Soy Milk) Broth (page 42)
Ponzu Sauce (page 60)

INGREDIENTS

3 cups (2 ounces, or 57 g) fresh spinach leaves

3 nasubi (Japanese eggplant), stemmed and sliced into large chunks

1 medium carrot, julienned

¼ large daikon radish, peeled and thinly sliced (or 6 small radishes, halved)

1 large negi (Japanese green onion; or 2 scallions), julienned

6 fresh shiso (Japanese basil) leaves, preferably red (or regular or Thai basil)

1 block (14 ounces, or 395 g) firm tofu, drained and cut into 1-inch (2.5 cm) cubes

18 ounces (509 g) prepared udon noodles, drained

2 quarts (1.9 L) Tonyu (Soy Milk) Broth (see Hot Tip)

Ponzu Sauce, for dipping

The steaming soy milk broth used in this hot pot makes it taste rich and creamy, even though it is both gluten- and dairy-free. The Ponzu Sauce (page 60) adds a punchy zest to the vegetables and perfectly cuts through the creaminess of the broth. Even though this is a vegetable-only hot pot, the eggplant and plump noodles make it hearty and filling. Any vegetables can be substituted depending on what's in season—just look for a variety that will give you different textures and colors. Since it's shabu-shabu style and everything just gets a quick dip for cooking, slice all the vegetables very thinly so they cook quickly.

INSTRUCTIONS

1. Arrange the vegetables, shiso, tofu, and noodles on platters. Place the platters on the table around the hot pot.

2. Heat a 4-quart (3.8 L) hot pot or large saucepan over medium-high heat (about 425°F, or 220°C, in an electric pot). Add the tonyu broth and bring to a boil.

3. Let guests add their own vegetables, shiso, tofu, and noodles, swishing back and forth in the hot broth until tender and cooked through, 1 to 2 minutes. As food is added, adjust the heat to maintain a low boil.

4. Serve with the ponzu sauce for dipping.

HOT TIP

This recipe is easy to scale up or down. Just make sure your hot pot is filled about halfway with broth. If the liquid reduces over time, add more.

YUDOFU (TOFU NABE)

SKILL LEVEL: Moderate • **PREP TIME:** 20 minutes • **COOK TIME:** 10 minutes • **YIELD:** 4 servings •
PREPARATION: Stovetop

INGREDIENTS

1 large piece (roughly 20 inches, or 50 cm, square) dried kombu

1 quart (960 ml) room-temperature water

⅔ cup (160 ml) shoyu (Japanese soy sauce)

½ teaspoon dried bonito flakes

2 blocks (14 ounces, or 395 g, each) firm silken tofu, drained and cut into four 2-inch (5 cm) cubes

3 large scallions, white and light green parts only, thinly sliced

This simple, authentic dish is another one I learned from my friend Kiko. She told me that *yudofu* was a famous nabe served to Emperor Kameyama at Nanzen-ji Temple, in Kyoto, one of the most important Zen Buddhist temples in all of Japan. The method for preparing this dish is very important: Use room-temperature water when soaking the kombu. If the water is warm or too hot, the kombu develops a slimy, bitter film. The light, kombu-steeped water is the foundation for this dish.

Keep an eye on the heat so the hot pot doesn't come to a boil. The silken tofu is very delicate and will fall apart if it's cooked at higher than a simmer. Since this is a simple dish with few ingredients, seek out the highest-quality tofu you can find, as it will make a big difference in texture and flavor. In Japan, there is a specific yudofu pan that's made with a container in the center for heating the shoyu-bonito sauce, but here it is placed directly in the hot pot to keep it warm.

INSTRUCTIONS

1. In a 4-quart (3.8 L) hot pot or large saucepan, cover the kombu with the water. Let soak for 20 minutes. Remove and discard the kombu.

2. In an 8-ounce (240 ml) ramekin, stir together the shoyu and bonito flakes. Set the ramekin in the center of the hot pot or saucepan, being careful not to let the kombu water spill into the ramekin. If necessary, remove some of the kombu water.

3. Arrange the tofu in the pot around the ramekin. Cook over medium heat (about 425°F, or 220°C, in an electric hot pot) until the tofu and the shoyu-bonito sauce are heated through, about 8 minutes.

4. Ladle a spoonful of the shoyu-bonito sauce into 4 shallow bowls and top each with a piece of tofu.

5. Garnish with the scallions.

SPECIALTY HOT POTS

MONGOLIAN LAMB HOT POT

SKILL LEVEL: Moderate • **PREP TIME:** 20 minutes • **COOK TIME:** 15 minutes • **YIELD:** 4 to 6 servings •
PREPARATION: Tableside

TO MAKE IN ADVANCE

Mongolian Broth (page 53)
Sesame Miso Sauce (page 63)
Steamed Japanese Rice (page 64)

INGREDIENTS

1 pound (454 g) boneless lamb, very
     thinly sliced (see Hot Tips)
3 baby bok choy, quartered
     lengthwise
4 ounces (113 g) gai lan (Chinese
     broccoli), washed and stemmed
3 ounces (85 g) enoki mushrooms,
     cleaned and trimmed
1 large tomato, cut into ½-inch-thick
     (13 mm) wedges and seeded
½ watermelon radish, peeled and
     thinly sliced on a mandoline
¼ small kabocha (Japanese
     pumpkin), with peel on, seeded
     and thinly sliced
4 rectangular pieces aburaage
     (fried tofu), sliced ¼ inch
     (6 mm) thick
1 block (14 ounces, or 395 g) firm
     silken tofu, drained and cut into
     1-inch (2.5 cm) pieces
1 pound (454 g) prepared ramen
     noodles, drained and divided into
     3-ounce (85 g) portions
2 quarts (1.9 L) Original or Spicy
     Mongolian Broth or 4 cups
     (960 ml) Original Mongolian
     Broth and 4 cups (960 ml) Spicy
     Mongolian Broth (see Hot Tips)
Steamed Japanese Rice, for serving
Sesame Miso Sauce, for dipping

Most Mongolian hot pot restaurants usually offer three options: original, spicy, or half-and-half. I always prefer a traditional split pot because it gives guests the freedom to choose. The aromatics in the broths complement the lamb and mellow any gaminess, while the Sesame Miso Sauce (page 63) is the perfect savory finish for both meat and vegetables.

INSTRUCTIONS

1. Arrange the lamb, vegetables, tofu, and noodles on platters. Place the platters on the table around the hot pot.

2. Heat a 4-quart (3.8 L) hot pot or large saucepan over medium-high heat (about 425°F, or 220°C, in an electric hot pot). Add the Mongolion broth. If you are using a split hot pot and serving both broths, repeat on the other side with the spicy Mongolian broth. Bring to a boil.

3. Let guests add their own lamb, vegetables, tofu, and noodles, swishing back and forth for a few minutes in the hot broth until each item is tender and cooked through. As food is added, adjust the heat to maintain a low boil.

4. Serve with the steamed rice on the side and the sesame miso sauce for dipping.

HOT TIPS

Freeze the lamb up to 4 hours until it is firm and easier to slice or purchase sukiyaki or shabu-shabu lamb at Asian markets or ask your butcher to thinly slice it.

This recipe is easy to scale up or down. Just make sure your hot pot is filled about halfway with broth. If the liquid reduces over time, add more.

TORI KAMO NABE (CHICKEN AND DUCK NABE)

SKILL LEVEL: Moderate • **PREP TIME:** 30 minutes, plus 2 hours marinating time • **COOK TIME:** 40 minutes • **YIELD:** 4 to 6 servings • **PREPARATION:** Stovetop

TO MAKE IN ADVANCE

Basic Dashi (page 28)
Sweet-and-Sour Layu Chili Sauce
(page 61)
Steamed Japanese Rice (page 64)

INGREDIENTS

1½ pounds (680 g) boneless skinless chicken thighs, cut into bite-size pieces
1 tablespoon (15 g) shoyu koji (see Hot Tip)
2 skin-on duck breasts (10 ounces, or 280 g, each)
Kosher salt, to taste
Freshly ground black pepper, to taste
1 medium shallot, thinly sliced
1 piece (1 inch, or 2.5 cm) fresh ginger, peeled and finely grated
2 large garlic cloves, minced
2 quarts (1.9 L) Basic Dashi (or dashi made with an instant mix)
¼ cup (60 ml) sake (rice wine)
¼ cup (60 ml) mirin (sweet rice wine)
1 tablespoon (15 ml) shoyu (Japanese soy sauce)
2 cups (about 5 ounces, or 140 g) packed very thinly sliced red cabbage
5 ounces (140 g) king trumpet mushrooms (or brown cremini mushrooms), cleaned, trimmed, and sliced lengthwise
1 large carrot, shaved into thin ribbons with a vegetable peeler
1 block (14 ounces, or 395 g) medium-firm tofu, drained and cut into 1-inch (2.5 cm) cubes

This light, clean broth really lets the flavor of the duck shine. Before gently simmering in the broth, the duck is cooked low and slow, keeping the meat juicy and tender—this also helps the fat render out and makes the skin extra crispy. The cooking process is simple, but it does require some patience: Start with the duck, skin side down, in a cold pan while you slowly turn up the heat. If you start with a hot pan or turn up the heat before the fat starts to render, a crust will form on the duck and you'll be left with a thick, chewy piece of duck skin. Don't discard the leftover duck fat in the skillet—it is repurposed for cooking the shallots, ginger, and garlic (and also adding more duck flavor to the soup). The Sweet-and-Sour Layu Chili Sauce (page 61) is not optional here; it makes for the perfect accompaniment to the poultry and the duck.

INSTRUCTIONS

1. In a small bowl, toss the chicken thighs with the shoyu koji. Cover and refrigerate for at least 2 hours. Pat the duck breasts dry with paper towels and season with salt and pepper.

2. In a cold medium nonstick skillet, place the duck, skin side down. Place the skillet over medium-low heat and cook, without turning, until the duck fat has rendered and the skin is beginning to brown, about 15 minutes. You should hear a low sizzle. If the fat starts to splatter, lower the heat.

3. Increase the heat to high and cook for 2 to 3 minutes more, until the skin is golden and caramelized. Transfer the duck to a cutting board and let rest for 10 minutes. Slice the breasts about ½ inch (13 mm) thick. The duck should still be slightly raw. Pour the duck fat into a small heatproof bowl and reserve.

4. In a 4-quart (3.8 L) hot pot or large saucepan over medium heat (about 400°F, or 200°C, in an electric pot), heat 2 tablespoons (30 ml) of the reserved duck fat. Add the shallot, ginger, and garlic. Cook for about 5 minutes, stirring occasionally, until the shallot is translucent.

1 pound (454 g) prepared black shirataki noodles, drained and divided into 3-ounce (85 g) portions
Shredded nori (seaweed), for garnishing
Steamed Japanese Rice, for serving
Sweet-and-Sour Layu Chili Sauce, for serving

5. Add the dashi, sake, mirin, and shoyu to the hot pot, and bring to a boil. Add the marinated chicken. Cover the pot, reduce the heat to low, and simmer for 5 minutes.

6. Add the vegetables, tofu, and noodles. Cover the pot and cook for 5 minutes more.

7. Lay the sliced duck over the top of the vegetables. Cook, covered, for about 2 minutes more, until the chicken is cooked through, the vegetables are tender, and the duck is slightly pink.

8. Ladle into shallow bowls and garnish with the shredded nori. Serve with the steamed rice on the side and the layu chili sauce for dipping.

HOT TIP

Shoyu koji is a savory condiment made of fermented rice and shoyu (Japanese soy sauce). You can find it at Asian markets and online. If you cannot find shoyu koji, season the chicken with salt and add 1 additional tablespoon (15 ml) shoyu to the dashi with the sake and mirin.

MEAT LOVER'S MACANESE HOT POT

SKILL LEVEL: Moderate • **PREP TIME:** 20 minutes • **COOK TIME:** 20 minutes • **YIELD:** 6 to 8 servings •
PREPARATION: Tableside

TO MAKE IN ADVANCE

Macanese Broth (page 58)
Chili-Cilantro-Lime Sauce (page 62)

INGREDIENTS

2 ounces (55 g) dried harusame
    cellophane noodles
Boiling water
8 ounces (227 g) Kobe, rib-eye, or
    Angus beef, very thinly sliced
    (see Hot Tips)
8 ounces (227 g) pork loin, very thinly
    sliced (see Hot Tips)
8 ounces (227 g) boneless, skinless
    chicken breast, very thinly sliced
    (see Hot Tips)
5 ounces (140 g) forest nameko
    mushrooms (or buna-shimeji
    or enoki mushrooms), cleaned,
    trimmed, and torn into small
    bunches
2 cups (60 g) packed baby spinach
1 block (14 ounces, or 395 g) firm
    tofu, drained and cut into 1-inch
    (2.5 cm) cubes
2 quarts (1.9 L) Macanese Broth (see
    Hot Tips)
2 ears fresh corn, shucked and cut
    into 2-inch (5 cm) pieces
Lime wedges, for garnishing
Fresh cilantro leaves, for garnishing
Thinly sliced Fresno peppers (or
    jalapeño peppers), for garnishing
Tahini, for serving
Chili-Cilantro-Lime Sauce,
    for serving

This hot pot was created by my friend Emily Lai and inspired by her family and their love of hot pots. Although she is Malaysian, this Macanese hot pot was a staple in her house growing up. She recalls that whenever her parents or aunts and uncles threw a party, it was always a hot pot party. It was not only an easy way for them to feed the whole family, but it also allowed for all the young cousins to help with the "cooking," as they dipped their food into the bubbling broth and served themselves. Emily's family liked to take their hot pot parties late into the evening—cooking, eating, drinking, chatting, breaking for a bit, and then repeating.

INSTRUCTIONS

1. Place the dried noodles in a large heatproof bowl and cover with boiling water. Let sit for about 10 minutes, until softened. Rinse under cold water, drain well, and cut in half.

2. Arrange the beef, pork, chicken, mushrooms, spinach, tofu, and noodles on platters. Place the platters on the table around the hot pot.

3. Heat a 4-quart (3.8 L) hot pot or large saucepan over medium-high heat (about 425°F, or 220°C, in an electric pot). Add the Macanese broth and corn, and bring to a boil.

4. Let guests add their own meat (beef, pork, or chicken), vegetables, tofu, and noodles, swishing back and forth in the hot broth until tender and cooked through, 1 to 2 minutes. As food is added, adjust the heat to maintain a low boil.

5. Serve with the lime wedges, cilantro, Fresno peppers, tahini, and the chili-cilantro-lime sauce, as desired.

HOT TIPS

Freeze the meat up to 4 hours until it is firm and easier to slice or purchase sukiyaki or shabu-shabu meat at Asian markets or ask your butcher to thinly slice it.

This recipe is easy to scale up or down. Just make sure your hot pot is filled about halfway with broth. If the liquid reduces over time, add more.

SIDE DISHES

CHICKEN DELICIOUS

SKILL LEVEL: Moderate • **PREP TIME:** 15 minutes, plus 2 to 8 hours marinating time • **COOK TIME:** 30 minutes •
YIELD: 6 to 8 servings

INGREDIENTS

6 tablespoons (90 ml) shoyu (Japanese soy sauce)

2 tablespoons (30 ml) agave nectar

2 tablespoons (30 ml) sake (rice wine)

1 piece (1½ inches, or 3.5 cm) fresh ginger, peeled and finely grated

2 large garlic cloves, minced

2 large scallions, white parts only, thinly sliced; green parts reserved for garnishing

½ teaspoon kosher salt

¼ teaspoon freshly ground black pepper

2½ pounds (1.1 kg), or 8 boneless, skinless chicken thighs, each cut into 4 or 5 uniform pieces

Vegetable oil, for frying

3½ cups (175 g) panko bread crumbs

2 large eggs

Lemon wedges, for garnishing

This recipe started as my attempt at making chicken *karaage*, the Japanese equivalent of fried chicken. It's dredged in *katakuriko* (Japanese potato starch) and deep-fried, twice. The result is fried chicken that stays shatteringly crunchy for hours. Because I believe frying chicken once is enough, and after much trial and error, the key ingredient turned out to be panko (Japanese bread crumbs). The true test—my kids loved this, gobbled it right up, and said, "Mom, this chicken is delicious!"

INSTRUCTIONS

1. In a medium bowl, whisk together the shoyu, agave, sake, ginger, garlic, scallions, salt, and pepper until smooth. Add the chicken to the marinade. Refrigerate to marinate for at least 2 hours or overnight.

2. Line a rimmed baking sheet with foil and place a cooling rack in it.

3. In a deep, straight-sided medium skillet, heat 2 inches (5 cm) of oil to 325°F (170°C). When the oil is hot, test the temperature by adding a small amount of panko to the hot oil—it should sizzle and brown up quickly when hot.

4. In a shallow bowl, beat the eggs. In a second shallow bowl, spread the panko in an even layer. Working with one piece of chicken at a time, tap off any excess marinade. Dip it into the egg and then cover it with panko. Set aside on a plate and repeat the dredging process with 3 to 5 more pieces of chicken.

5. Carefully distribute the pieces of breaded chicken in the hot oil and fry until golden brown on both sides, 3 to 4 minutes. While the chicken fries, bread a second batch of 4 to 6 pieces. Using a slotted spoon, transfer the cooked chicken to the prepared cooling rack, making sure none are touching. Allow the oil to come back up to temperature and fry the next batch of chicken. Repeat this process until all the chicken is cooked.

6. Serve warm or at room temperature and garnish with lemon wedges and the green parts of the scallion.

SIMPLE SALAD WITH SESAME SOY DRESSING

SKILL LEVEL: Easy • **PREP TIME:** 10 minutes • **YIELD:** 4 servings

INGREDIENTS

¼ cup (60 ml) rice vinegar

¼ cup (68 g) shiro (white) miso

2 tablespoons (16 g) toasted white sesame seeds, plus more for garnishing

3 tablespoons (45 g) packed light brown sugar

¼ cup (60 ml) sesame oil

Kosher salt, to taste

½ large head iceberg lettuce, cored and thinly sliced

1 medium carrot, shredded

½ ripe Asian pear, peeled, cored, and julienned

1 avocado, halved, pitted, peeled, and thinly sliced

My kids are like most: they don't like "salads made with weeds," which translates to, "We will only eat iceberg or romaine lettuce." So, I created this simple salad that they really enjoy. My son, Ryan, still eats it plain without any dressing, but most kids will enjoy the sweetness of the Asian pear and the savory creaminess of the miso. The dressing is also a fantastic dip for crudités or drizzled over half an avocado for a quick snack. You'll have enough dressing for multiple uses, so store it in a jar and keep it on hand in the refrigerator. It will last for a few weeks.

INSTRUCTIONS

1. In a small bowl, whisk together the vinegar, miso, sesame seeds, and brown sugar until smooth. While whisking constantly, slowly stream in the sesame oil until incorporated. Season with salt.

2. Arrange the lettuce, carrot, pear, and avocado on salad plates and drizzle with some of the dressing. Garnish with more sesame seeds.

BROILED MOCHI WITH DASHI (AKEMOCHI)

SKILL LEVEL: Moderate • **PREP TIME:** 20 minutes • **COOK TIME:** 10 minutes • **YIELD:** 6 servings

TO MAKE IN ADVANCE

Basic Dashi (page 28)

INGREDIENTS

Nonstick cooking spray, for preparing the baking sheet

6 kiri mochi (pounded rice cakes) blocks or freshly made maru mochi (mochi patties), halved (see Hot Tips)

2 cups Basic Dashi (or dashi made with an instant mix)

¼ cup (60 ml) shoyu (Japanese soy sauce)

1 piece (2 inches, or 5 cm) fresh ginger, peeled and finely grated

1 tablespoon (6 g) finely grated peeled daikon (Japanese radish)

Shredded nori (seaweed), for garnishing

1 large scallion, white and light green parts only, thinly sliced, for garnishing

Carrot flowers, for garnishing (optional; see Hot Tips)

HOT TIPS

Mochi can be found fresh and packaged at most Asian markets, typically in the freezer section. Unlike dessert mochi, this mochi is not flavored, colored, or filled with anything.

To make carrot flowers, peel one large carrot and slice it ⅛ inch (3 mm) thick. Using a paring knife, cut small notches around the edge of each slice to make it look like a flower.

Since I was a kid, it has been our New Year's Eve tradition to make freshly pounded mochi (a dense cake or paste made from ground *mochigome*, or Japanese short-grain rice) and then eat it hot, puffed, and golden on New Year's Day morning. The best, and easiest, way to do this is to pop it under the broiler. The mochi becomes light and crispy on the outside and gooey on the inside, and reminds me of sitting around the table with my siblings, fighting over who gets the last one. The mochi almost doubles in size under the broiler and I have such clear memories of staring at it, watching it grow, and eagerly waiting for my mom to pull it from the oven. This is still an integral part of my family's New Year's routine. These days, I doctor it up with a simple dashi broth with grated ginger, daikon, and scallion and serve the crispy mochi floating in the soup like matzo balls. I like to eat the broth-soaked mochi first, and then sip the remaining soup right from the bowl.

INSTRUCTIONS

1. Preheat the broiler and arrange a rack 5 inches (13 cm) from the heat. Line a rimmed baking sheet with aluminum foil and coat with nonstick cooking spray.

2. Arrange the mochi on the prepared baking sheet, leaving 2 inches (5 cm) between each piece. Broil until the mochi doubles in size and is puffy and golden brown, about 5 minutes. You do not need to turn the mochi.

3. In a small saucepan over high heat, combine the dashi, shoyu, ginger, and daikon, and bring to a boil. Reduce the heat to low and simmer, uncovered, for 2 minutes.

4. Ladle ½ cup (120 ml) of the hot dashi broth into 6 small bowls. Top each bowl with 2 pieces of broiled mochi and garnish with nori, scallion, and carrot flowers (if using).

COMPRESSED SPINACH SALAD WITH SESAME SAUCE (GOMA-AE)

SKILL LEVEL: Easy • **PREP TIME:** 10 minutes • **COOK TIME:** 10 minutes • **YIELD:** 4 servings

INGREDIENTS

2 tablespoons (16 g) white sesame seeds, plus more for garnishing

1 tablespoon (15 ml) shoyu (Japanese soy sauce)

1 teaspoon sugar

3 tablespoons (45 ml) sesame oil, divided

1 pound (454 g) fresh spinach (not baby spinach), cleaned and trimmed

In Japanese cooking, *goma-ae* refers to any dish where a vegetable is mixed with a sesame-based sauce. The sweet-and-salty dressing, which typically includes sugar and soy sauce, goes well with most vegetables, but this simple spinach version is probably the one I make the most. For the best results, I encourage you to grind your own sesame seeds, but you can also find tubes of ground sesame paste at most Asian markets, or substitute tahini.

INSTRUCTIONS

1. In a small skillet over low heat, toast the sesame seeds for about 10 minutes, until fragrant and golden brown, constantly stirring or swirling the seeds in the pan as they cook. Let cool, then transfer to a mortar with a pestle or clean coffee grinder. Crush the toasted sesame seeds into a fine powder (see Hot Tip).

2. In a medium bowl, stir together the crushed sesame seeds, shoyu, and sugar—it should look like a thick paste.

3. Heat 1 tablespoon (15 ml) of the sesame oil in a large skillet over medium-high heat. Add one-third of the spinach and cook for about 3 minutes, stirring, until just wilted. Transfer to a colander set over a bowl. Repeat 2 more times with the remaining sesame oil and spinach. Let the spinach cool.

4. Once cool enough to handle, use your hands to squeeze out any liquid from the spinach. Add the spinach to the bowl with the dressing and toss to coat. Refrigerate until cooled and ready to serve.

5. Using your hands, squeeze the spinach into 4 tight balls and arrange on 4 small plates. Garnish with sesame seeds and serve.

6. The sesame dressing can be made ahead and stored in the refrigerator for up to 3 days.

HOT TIP

If you use a coffee grinder, be careful not to overprocess the seeds or you'll end up with sesame paste. Stop grinding before the seeds start to release oil or the powder will clump.

JAPANESE MUSHROOM TOAST

SKILL LEVEL: Easy • **PREP TIME:** 10 minutes • **COOK TIME:** 15 minutes • **YIELD:** 4 to 6 servings

INGREDIENTS

1 tablespoon (14 g) unsalted butter

3 tablespoons (45 ml) olive oil, divided

1 medium shallot, finely chopped

12 ounces (340 g) mixed Japanese mushrooms, cleaned, trimmed, and chopped

1 tablespoon (15 ml) sesame oil

Kosher salt, to taste

1 small French bread or rustic loaf, sliced diagonally ½ inch (13 mm) thick

1 tablespoon (17 g) shiro (white) miso

1 teaspoon shoyu (Japanese soy sauce)

¼ teaspoon shichimi togarashi (or red pepper flakes)

1 large scallion, white and light green parts only, thinly sliced

After a week of creating different sukiyaki recipes, I ended up with a pile of leftover Japanese mushrooms. Back when we lived in London, I enjoyed all the lovely breakfast places with toasts heaped with different vegetables and savory meats, but my favorite was always a toast overflowing with rich, sautéed wild mushrooms. This recipe is in memory of our time there, but with a little Japanese twist. Here, I use shiitake, king trumpets, oyster, and forest nameko mushrooms, and hit them with a bit of savory-sweet miso and spicy shichimi togarashi powder. Any leftover mushrooms will work here, but the flavor will be more complex with a mix of varieties. These crunchy toasts work as a light lunch, topped with an over-easy egg for breakfast, or halved on the diagonal and served with cocktails.

INSTRUCTIONS

1. Preheat the broiler and arrange a rack 6 inches (15 cm) from the heat. Line a plate with paper towels and set aside.

2. In a medium skillet over medium-high heat, melt the butter with 1 tablespoon (15 ml) of the olive oil. Add the shallot. Cook for about 1 minute, stirring, until softened. Add the mushrooms. Cook, stirring occasionally, until tender and browned, about 8 minutes. Stir in the sesame oil. Season lightly with salt and transfer to the prepared plate to drain.

3. Meanwhile, brush the bread with the remaining 2 tablespoons (30 ml) olive oil. Arrange the slices on a rimmed baking sheet and broil, turning once, until golden brown, about 5 minutes.

4. In a small bowl, whisk together the miso, shoyu, and shichimi togarashi. Fold in the mushrooms.

5. Spoon the mushrooms onto the toasts and garnish with the scallion.

SHISHITO PEPPER TEMPURA

SKILL LEVEL: Easy • **PREP TIME:** 10 minutes • **COOK TIME:** 20 minutes • **YIELD:** 4 to 6 servings

INGREDIENTS

Vegetable oil, for frying
1 tablespoon (15 ml) shichimi togarashi (Japanese chile pepper)
1 tablespoon (15 ml) kosher salt
1 cup (120 g) all-purpose flour
1 cup (240 ml) water
3 ice cubes
8 ounces (227 g) shishito peppers

Tempura is my favorite thing to serve alongside hot pots, because the crunchy texture adds dimension to the soft, stewed meats and vegetables. A trick I learned while growing up and working at Mom's Sushi Bar in Fullerton, California, was to get the tempura batter really cold before frying by adding ice cubes to it. When the cold batter is added to the hot oil, it puffs into a light, crisp coating without burning. I use shishito peppers in this recipe because they are perfectly bite-size and only mildly spicy—even kids will eat them. Be careful, though; they do say that one out of every ten shishito peppers is extra spicy. I say make a game of it: First one to get the spicy pepper does the dishes?

INSTRUCTIONS

1. Line a plate with paper towels and set aside.

2. Fill a large saucepan or deep-fryer with 1½ inches (3.5 cm) of vegetable oil and heat over medium-high heat to 360°F (182°C).

3. In a small bowl, stir together the shichimi togarashi and kosher salt. Set aside.

4. In a medium bowl, whisk together the flour and water until smooth. Add the ice cubes to the batter to keep it cold, whisking the batter as the ice cubes melt.

5. Test the oil by adding a very small amount of batter—it should fry up quickly when hot enough.

6. When the oil is hot, add a small handful of shishito peppers to the batter and toss to coat. One by one, add the battered peppers to the oil. Fry for about 5 minutes, until lightly browned. Using a slotted spoon, transfer the fried peppers to the prepared plate to drain and sprinkle with the togarashi-salt mixture. Repeat with the remaining shishito peppers.

7. Serve immediately.

SHIO KOJI PICKLED VEGETABLES

SKILL LEVEL: Easy • **PREP TIME:** 10 minutes, plus 2 hours marinating time • **YIELD:** 4 to 6 servings

INGREDIENTS

6 tablespoons (90 g) shio koji

¼ cup (60 ml) fresh lemon juice

2 teaspoons freshly grated lemon zest

1 tablespoon (15 ml) sugar

1 teaspoon peppercorns

10 whole cloves

2 dried bay leaves

½ teaspoon red pepper flakes

2 large carrots, peeled and thinly sliced on the diagonal

2 large radishes, thinly sliced on a mandoline

1 cup (4 ounces, or 113 g) peeled and thinly sliced (on a mandoline) daikon (Japanese radish),

1 cup (4 ounces, or 113 g) peeled and thinly sliced (on a mandoline) jicama

½ English cucumber, peeled, seeded, and thinly sliced

8 fresh shiso (Japanese basil) leaves, halved down the middle

One day at a Japanese market here in Boulder, I met a woman named Miko, who offered to make me some of her homemade shio koji, an umami-rich condiment made from shio (salt) and rice that is fermented with koji, the edible fungus used to make miso and sake. It's perfect with raw vegetables, because it helps bring out their natural sweetness. These quick pickles are best eaten within a couple of hours when the shio koji flavor is stronger and the vegetables haven't released too much liquid. And though you may not know someone like Miko, you can easily find shio koji at Japanese markets and online.

INSTRUCTIONS

1. In a medium bowl, stir together the shio koji, lemon juice and zest, sugar, peppercorns, cloves, bay leaves, and red pepper flakes.

2. Add the vegetables and shiso, and toss to coat.

3. Refrigerate to marinate for at least 2 hours or up to overnight before serving.

MOM'S PORK WONTONS

SKILL LEVEL: Moderate • **PREP TIME:** 40 minutes • **COOK TIME:** 30 minutes • **YIELD:** Makes 50 to 60 wontons

INGREDIENTS

Sweet-and-Sour Sauce

½ cup (120 ml) low-sodium chicken broth (store-bought is fine to use here)

2 tablespoons (30 ml) cornstarch

¾ cup (120 g) finely chopped pineapple (or 1 can, 6 ounces, or 170 g, crushed pineapple), drained

½ cup (100 g) sugar

½ cup (120 g) ketchup

¼ cup (60 ml) rice wine vinegar

Pork Wontons

8 ounces (227 g) ground pork

8 ounces (227 g) large shrimp (6 to 8 shrimp), shelled and deveined

1 large egg

½ cup (62 g) water chestnuts, drained

3 scallions, white and light green parts only

1 piece (1½ inches, or 3.5 cm) fresh ginger, peeled

1 large shiitake mushroom, stemmed

1 small garlic clove

1 tablespoon (4 g) fresh parsley

1 teaspoon kosher salt

½ teaspoon freshly ground black pepper

1 package (12 ounces, or 340 g) wonton wrappers (or round gyoza or potsticker wrappers)

Vegetable oil, for frying

My mom and her best friend, Tucky, used to make these wontons for our church's food festival, prepping thousands of them ahead of time and freezing them between layers of wax paper. I remember being in the church banquet hall, filled with tables, and it seemed like the entire congregation was there to help. I'd sit with my brother, sister, and cousins happily making wontons for hours. When wontons are defrosted, they can become soggy, so my mom and Tucky had a trick for their filling: instead of using regular onions (which weep when thawed), they used scallions. This recipe freezes well, so I highly recommend making the full batch of wontons even if you don't plan to eat them right away.

Also, the great part about this recipe is that these wontons can be fried and served with a dipping sauce or simmered in a hot pot—it just comes down to how you assemble them. Fried wontons are folded to look like a boat with two sails and simmered wontons look like a cinched-up purse. The boat shape limits the filling to less meat, so the filling is able to cook through during the brief frying time; however, the cinched-up purse can hold more filling because the wontons can simmer for a longer time. If you want to try these in a soup, check out my Pork Wontons with Macanese Broth Hot Pot (page 72), where the wontons are cooked in a slightly sweet, aromatic pork bone broth until perfectly tender.

INSTRUCTIONS

1. **To make the sweet-and-sour sauce:** In a small saucepan, whisk together the chicken broth and cornstarch to make a slurry. Add the remaining sauce ingredients and whisk until smooth.

2. Place the saucepan over medium-low heat and bring the sauce to a simmer. Cook, whisking, until the sugar dissolves and the sauce is slightly thickened, about 10 minutes.

3. **To make the pork wontons:** In a food processor, combine the pork, shrimp, egg, water chestnuts, scallions, ginger, mushroom, garlic, parsley, salt, and pepper. Pulse until well combined and a meatball-like texture is formed. If you do not have a food processor, finely chop the ingredients and mix to combine.

(continued on page 150)

HOT TIP

If preparing these wontons to use in a hot pot, place 1 rounded tablespoon (14 g) of filling in the center of a wonton square. Moisten the outside of the square with water and pinch up the opposite edges to make a square purse with sealed edges.

4. **To assemble the wontons:** Fill a small bowl with water and line a large airtight container with wax or parchment paper.

5. Working with 1 wonton wrapper at a time, place a rounded teaspoon of filling in the center of the wrapper. Be careful not to overstuff the wonton wrappers or they will be difficult to seal.

6. Wet your finger in the bowl of water and moisten the wrapper around the filling. Fold the bottom half of the wrapper up and away from you so the corners of the square are offset. Gently press the wonton wrapper together around the filling to seal. (If you are making these wontons for a hot pot, see Hot Tip.)

7. Transfer to the airtight container and repeat with the remaining filling and wonton wrappers, separating each layer of prepared wontons with wax or parchment paper.

8. Fill a large saucepan or a deep-fryer with 1½ inches (3.5 cm) of vegetable oil and heat over medium-high heat to 350°F (177°C). Line a rimmed baking sheet with paper towels. When the oil is hot, test the temperature by adding a small piece of wonton wrapper to the oil—it should fry up quickly when hot.

9. Working in small batches, carefully add the wontons to the hot oil. They should not be touching. Fry for about 5 minutes, until puffed, crispy, and lightly browned. Using a slotted spoon, transfer the fried wontons to the paper towel–lined baking sheet to drain. Repeat with the remaining wontons.

10. Serve while hot with the sweet-and-sour sauce for dipping.

11. These wontons can be made ahead and frozen for up to 1 month. You can also refrigerate them overnight and fry them the next day, but don't refrigerate them for longer than that.

AVOCADO WITH BLACK SESAME AND SHOYU KOJI

SKILL LEVEL: Moderate • **PREP TIME:** 10 minutes • **YIELD:** 4 to 6 servings

INGREDIENTS

¼ cup (60 ml) rice wine vinegar (or apple cider vinegar)

¼ cup (60 ml) mirin (sweet rice wine)

4 teaspoons (20 g) shoyu koji

2 teaspoons black sesame seeds

¼ cup (60 ml) sesame oil

4 medium firm-ripe avocados, halved, pitted, peeled, and cut into bite-size pieces

Crispy onions (such as Lars Own brand), for garnishing

Furikake, for garnishing

The shoyu koji in this dish is unique and savory, and inspired the dressing used here. Shoyu koji also adds instant umami to meat, fish, or vegetables in marinades or sauces, and is a more flavorful substitute for salt. This is one of my favorite sides because it's so addictive and versatile. Eat the marinated avocado on its own, toss in salads, or roll in a sheet of Roasted Nori (page 65) with some steamed rice for a snack. Also, I garnish the salad with crispy onions and furikake, a Japanese spice mixture, but you could also sprinkle the avocado with thinly sliced roasted nori or thinly sliced garlic crisped in some hot oil.

INSTRUCTIONS

1. In a medium bowl, whisk together the vinegar, mirin, shoyu koji, and sesame seeds.

2. While whisking, slowly drizzle in the sesame oil until incorporated.

3. Gently fold in the avocado.

4. Transfer to bowls and garnish with the crispy onions and furikake.

KOREAN SCALLION PANCAKES

SKILL LEVEL: Easy • **PREP TIME:** 20 minutes • **COOK TIME:** 20 minutes • **YIELD:** Makes 24 pancakes

INGREDIENTS

Batter

2 cups (240 g) cake flour
1 teaspoon baking powder
1 teaspoon kosher salt
½ teaspoon freshly ground black
    pepper
2 cups (475 ml) chilled club soda,
    plus more as needed
2 large eggs
1 tablespoon (32 g) gochujang
    (Korean chili paste)
1 bunch scallions (approximately
    10 stalks), thinly sliced on the bias
¼ cup (12 g) snipped fresh chives
¼ cup (36 g) toasted sesame seeds
Vegetable oil, for frying

Dipping Sauce

¼ cup (60 ml) shoyu (Japanese soy
    sauce)
¼ cup (60 ml) rice wine vinegar
¼ cup (70 g) sweet chili sauce
2 teaspoons sesame oil

Garnish

Flaky sea salt
Fresh chive blossoms, (optional)

These Korean-style scallion pancakes have a tender center and crunchy edges. The effervescence of the club soda reacts with the baking powder for a light and airy batter that translates to an ethereally crisp crust. I prefer to make smaller pancakes for a neat finger food and crispier edges.

INSTRUCTIONS

1. **To make the batter:** In a medium bowl, whisk together the flour, baking powder, salt, and pepper. In another medium bowl, whisk together the club soda, eggs, and gochujang. Whisk the wet ingredients into the dry ingredients, being careful not to overmix. Chill for 15 minutes.

2. **To make the dipping sauce:** In a small bowl, whisk together all the dipping sauce ingredients.

3. Preheat the oven to 200°F (93°C). Set a cooling rack in a rimmed baking sheet and place it on the middle rack of the oven. Remove the batter from the refrigerator and gently fold in the scallions, chives, and sesame seeds. The pancake batter should have a thin consistency; if the batter is too thick, add more club soda, ¼ cup (60 ml) at a time, and mix well. You are looking for a thin pancake batter consistency.

4. Heat 2 tablespoons (30 ml) of vegetable oil in a medium skillet over medium-high heat. Add the batter in 2-tablespoon (30 ml) mounds to the pan and cook until crisp and golden brown, about 1 minute per side. Transfer to the rack in the oven to keep warm. Repeat with the remaining batter, adding vegetable oil to the pan for each batch.

5. Arrange the scallion pancakes on a platter and sprinkle with the flaky sea salt and chive blossoms, if using. Serve immediately with the dipping sauce.

HOT TIP

Cake flour is finer in texture and has a lower protein content (therefore less gluten) than all-purpose flour, so when used, it gives a more delicate texture and a better rise. If you want to make cake flour, use 1 cup (120 g) all-purpose flour minus 2 tablespoons (16 g), plus 2 tablespoons (16 g) cornstarch, for 1 cup (120 g) cake flour.

DESSERTS

YUZU CITRUS SORBET

SKILL LEVEL: Moderate • **PREP TIME:** 35 minutes, plus 4 hours freezing time • **YIELD:** 8 servings

INGREDIENTS

4 cups (800 g) sugar

4 cups (940 ml) water

1 cup (240 ml) yuzu juice (from 8 fresh small yuzu or bottled, or the juice of 4 small lemons and 4 small limes)

1½ tablespoons (9 g) freshly grated orange zest

Fresh mint leaves, for garnishing

When I was younger, my mom used to throw these fabulous dinner parties with her friends, complete with the finest china, silver, and beautiful printed menus. The women who threw these elaborate suppers called themselves The Dames. I remember one evening when my mom let me have a taste of a lemon sorbet that they were serving in cutout lemon baskets—I'll never forget it. She told me it was to cleanse the palate between courses, and I thought it was the most sophisticated and special thing I'd ever eaten. This sorbet is my tribute to The Dames. Here, I use yuzu citrus instead of lemon. It has a fantastic tart taste that walks the line between lemon and lime (plus a touch of fresh orange zest for good measure). While I might not serve this in a hand-carved citrus basket, I still think they would approve.

INSTRUCTIONS

1. Prepare a large ice bath.

2. In a medium saucepan over medium-high heat, whisk together the sugar and water. Bring to a boil. Cook for about 5 minutes, whisking, until the sugar dissolves. Carefully pour the hot syrup into a medium bowl and set the bowl in the ice bath to cool, whisking every 5 minutes until completely cooled, about 20 minutes in all.

3. Remove the bowl from the ice bath and stir in the yuzu juice and orange zest. Pour the sorbet base into a 9 x 13-inch (23 x 33 cm) baking dish and transfer it to the freezer. Freeze the sorbet, stirring the mixture every hour with a fork, until set, soft, and smooth, at least 4 hours.

4. Scoop the sorbet into small bowls, garnish with the mint leaves, and serve right away.

EMIKO'S COFFEE ADZUKI KANTEN

SKILL LEVEL: Moderate • **PREP TIME:** 20 minutes, plus 5 to 6 hours refrigeration time • **YIELD:** Makes 48 squares

INGREDIENTS

Nonstick cooking spray, for preparing the pan
8 packets (¼ ounce, or 7 g, each) powdered gelatin
1¼ cups (300 ml) ice water
4½ cups (1 L) boiling water
¼ cup (60 ml) strong coffee, or 1 teaspoon instant coffee
2 cans (14 ounces, or 420 ml, each) sweetened condensed milk
1 can (16 ounces, or 454 g) tsubushian (sweetened adzuki red beans)

In my family, we ring in the New Year with a big traditional Japanese feast, but I always leave room for this dessert from my cousin Emiko. The sweet, earthy adzuki beans settle to the bottom, forming dramatic layers (with the help of the gelatin), and the hit of mocha makes this the perfect bite after a big meal. The recipe makes a lot and the dessert is on the sweet side, so just a small square per person is perfect.

INSTRUCTIONS

1. Coat a 9 x 13-inch (23 x 33 cm) pan with cooking spray. Set aside.

2. In a large bowl, combine the gelatin and ice water. Let sit until softened, about 5 minutes.

3. Add the boiling water to the gelatin and stir until dissolved.

4. Stir in the coffee, sweetened condensed milk, and tsubushian. Pour the mixture into the prepared pan, giving it a little shake to make sure the mixture is evenly distributed. You want the beans to be evenly distributed throughout the bottom of the pan. Refrigerate until set, about 5 hours or overnight.

5. Cut the custard into 1¼-inch (3 cm) squares and serve, flipping each piece over so the beans are on top.

CHOCOLATE COCONUT MOCHI CAKE

SKILL LEVEL: Moderate • **PREP TIME:** 30 minutes • **COOK TIME:** 45 minutes • **YIELD:** 18 to 20 servings

INGREDIENTS

Nonstick cooking spray, for preparing the pan

2 cups (280 g) mochiko (Japanese sweet rice flour)

½ cup (60 g) cake flour (see Hot Tip)

½ cup (43 g) unprocessed cocoa powder

1 teaspoon baking soda

½ teaspoon kosher salt

2 cups (480 ml) whole milk

1 can (13.5 ounces, or 405 ml) coconut milk

½ cup (140 g) melted dark, unsweetened chocolate, cooled slightly

1 teaspoon vanilla extract

5 large eggs, lightly beaten

½ cup (1 stick, or 112 g) salted butter, at room temperature

2 cups (450 g) packed dark brown sugar

Confectioners' sugar, for dusting

Ice cream, for serving

HOT TIP

Cake flour is finer in texture and has a lower protein content (therefore less gluten) than all-purpose flour, so when used, it gives a more delicate texture and a better rise. If you want to make cake flour, use 1 cup (120 g) all-purpose flour minus 2 tablespoons (16 g), plus 2 tablespoons (16 g) cornstarch, for 1 cup (120 g) cake flour.

Mochiko is a glutinous rice flour made from *mochigome* (a short-grain Japanese rice). The mochiko in this cake gives it more density and moisture, while the cake flour and baking soda help it rise like a traditional cake. But, there's nothing traditional about it—the result is a rich, not-too-sweet, chocolatey confection that sticks to your fork and is somewhere between a brownie and a cake. My family prefers it heated a bit and served with a scoop of vanilla ice cream.

INSTRUCTIONS

1. Preheat the oven to 350°F (180°C). Coat a 9 x 13-inch (23 x 33 cm) pan with cooking spray. Set aside.

2. In a medium bowl, whisk together the mochiko, cake flour, cocoa powder, baking soda, and salt.

3. In a separate medium bowl, whisk together the whole milk, coconut milk, melted chocolate, vanilla, and eggs until smooth.

4. In the bowl of a stand mixer fitted with the paddle attachment or in a large bowl and using a handheld electric mixer, cream the butter and brown sugar until light and fluffy, 3 to 4 minutes. Scrape down the sides.

5. With the mixer running, gradually add the dry and wet ingredients, alternating, until the batter is smooth and everything is just incorporated. Pour the batter into the prepared pan and smooth the top.

6. Bake for 40 to 45 minutes, until a toothpick inserted into the center comes out clean. Let cool in the pan for about 30 minutes.

7. Cut into thin slices and transfer to plates. Dust with the confectioners' sugar and serve with the ice cream.

STRAWBERRY-ROSE MOCHI

SKILL LEVEL: Easy • **PREP TIME:** 5 minutes • **COOK TIME:** 10 minutes • **YIELD:** Makes 18 to 24 round patties

INGREDIENTS

¼ cup (16 g) small, dried, edible rosebuds (see Hot Tip)

¼ cup (45 g) katakuriko (Japanese potato starch) or (32 g) cornstarch

1 cup (160 g) mochiko (Japanese sweet rice flour)

1 cup (200 g) sugar

1 teaspoon strawberry-flavored gelatin, preferably organic

¼ teaspoon rose water

1 cup (240 ml) water

HOT TIP

It is important to have freshly dried rosebuds, as older ones can be less fragrant. Try to get your rosebuds from a quality tea provider if you can't find fresh ones online.

I love the sweet and floral combination of the strawberry gelatin and the crushed rose petals, but this recipe is easy to riff on. Try lime-flavored gelatin with some finely grated lime zest or mango gelatin with a dusting of chili powder—go wherever your imagination takes you.

When forming mochi, my mom taught me it's essential to do it while the mochi paste is still piping hot. Because of this, I think I've burned off all my finger pads over the years. To avoid doing the same, I recommend kitchen gloves—this will make the mochi a little easier to handle. Although I don't normally use a microwave, it is the easiest and most efficient way of making this. If you don't have a microwave, you could also make this in a medium saucepan over medium heat. While working, you're looking for a soft and smooth consistency that is chewy and slightly sweet. Serve the mochi at the end of a meal or as a snack with a cup of hot green tea.

INSTRUCTIONS

1. In a mini food processor or clean coffee grinder, pulse the rosebuds with the katakuriko until finely ground. Spread in a shallow bowl.

2. In a medium microwave-safe bowl, whisk together the mochiko, sugar, gelatin, rose water, and water until smooth. Cover with plastic wrap and microwave on high power for 3 minutes. Stir with a spatula, scraping down the sides. Microwave for 3 minutes more, or until thickened and all the liquid is absorbed.

3. Working in batches and wearing kitchen gloves, dip your fingers in the rose-katakuriko powder and pinch off a Ping-Pong–size ball of the hot mochi. Toss it in the rose-katakuriko powder, shaking off any excess. Holding the mochi in one hand, fold the edges of the mochi underneath itself using your other hand, while rotating it clockwise and forming a 1½- to 2-inch (3.5 to 5 cm) patty with a smooth top. Transfer to a plate and repeat with the remaining mochi.

4. Toss the cooled mochi with any remaining rose-katakuriko powder and serve.

5. The prepared mochi can be made ahead and refrigerated for up to 3 days, but it is best eaten the day of preparation.

COCONUT-MATCHA CUSTARD WITH BERRIES

SKILL LEVEL: Easy • **PREP TIME:** 30 minutes, plus 4 hours refrigeration time • **YIELD:** 8 servings

INGREDIENTS

2 cans (14 ounces, or 414 ml, each) full-fat coconut milk

2½ teaspoons gelatin (about one ¼-ounce, or 7 g, package)

½ cup (161 g) maple syrup

1 teaspoon vanilla extract

2 teaspoons culinary-grade matcha powder

2 cups (250 g) fresh mixed berries (such as raspberries and blackberries)

½ cup (40 g) toasted unsweetened shredded coconut

Small mint sprigs, for garnishing

With so many foods chock-full of sugar, this dessert is truly good for the heart. It's gluten-free, has no refined sugar, and is loaded with beneficial antioxidants from the *matcha* tea. Matcha in powdered form is available in Asian markets and online, and you will find a wide price range. For the purposes of this recipe, you don't have to buy it at a premium. The consistency of the custard is light and smooth; the berries give it a delicate tartness, and the crunch of the shredded coconut makes you want to keep digging in for more. This dessert can easily be made ahead of time—make the day before, then pull it out of the fridge when you're ready to serve. Just allow for the four hours the gelatin needs to set. Garnish with the berries, coconut, and mint sprigs right before serving.

INSTRUCTIONS

1. Arrange eight 8-ounce (240 ml) ramekins on a small rimmed baking sheet.

2. In a small saucepan, whisk together the coconut milk and gelatin. Let sit for 5 minutes.

3. Whisk in the maple syrup, vanilla, and matcha. Place the pan over medium-low heat and bring to a gentle simmer. Do not let the custard boil. Once the gelatin completely dissolves, remove from the heat.

4. Using a fine-mesh sieve, strain the custard into the ramekins, filling them about three-quarters full. Transfer the baking sheet to the refrigerator and let the custards cool until set, at least 4 hours.

5. To serve, top each custard with the berries and toasted coconut and garnish with the mint.

HOT POT GLOSSARY

(Note: Most of these ingredients can be found at Asian markets or online.)

Adzuki beans: Sweet, small red beans used in many Japanese desserts and candies. Canned varieties are fine to use.

Bonito flakes: One of two ingredients used to make dashi stock and an essential in any Japanese pantry. Although they are made from dried bonito fish, they are mild in flavor and can be used as a condiment.

Daikon: A large, long, white radish with a mellow flavor that can be eaten raw, cooked, or pickled. It's normally quite large so you generally only need to use a portion for hot pots. Daikon adds a slight spiciness to any dressing or sauce and can also be used alone as a condiment. Use Western radish as a substitute.

Daikon sprouts: Sprouts that grow from a daikon plant. They have a slight peppery flavor and are often used in salads, sashimi, and soups. They can be eaten cooked or raw and can be added directly to a hot pot or used as a garnish.

Dashi: Japanese stock used as the base for many soups and dipping sauces. It is typically made with water, bonito flakes, and kombu. It is a fundamental Japanese ingredient and can also be found in concentrated powders or tea bags, with no MSG, that you can easily mix with water.

Enoki mushrooms: Beautiful, stark-white mushrooms that come in bunches attached at the bottom with long stems and tiny caps. They are mild in flavor and tender yet hold up when cooked in broth. They go well with anything. Use white button mushrooms as a substitute.

Furikake: A Japanese seasoning with seaweed, sesame seeds, sugar, and salt. It's commonly sprinkled over rice.

Gai lan: Chinese broccoli with thick stems and dark green leaves, both of which are edible. Similar to Western broccoli in flavor, this ingredient pairs well with fattier proteins as a nice contrast in texture and added freshness. Use Western broccoli as a substitute.

Ginger: Lemony, sharp, spicy, and sweet, ginger is a versatile root that can be used in cooked dishes and dressings, and as a condiment. Fresh ginger is widely available so there should never be a need to substitute the powdered variety.

Haiga rice: Medium brown rice best described as between a white and a brown rice, with a nutty flavor and light and fluffy texture. Unlike brown rice, haiga rice has the rice bran removed, so the result is a more tender grain when cooked.

Harusame noodles: Cellophane noodles made from potatoes and that look like translucent sticks. Most varieties need to be hydrated in lukewarm water for 10 minutes before being cooked briefly in the hot pot broth. Use vermicelli noodles as a substitute.

Kabocha: This Japanese pumpkin is small and stout, with a dark green outside and brightly colored orange-yellow flesh. Its taste is similar to a sweet potato. Kabocha peel tenderizes and is edible once cooked. Use sweet potato as a substitute.

Kabu: This Japanese white turnip is a bit larger than the Western turnip and is enjoyed raw or cooked. It is ideal for hot pots because it can be cooked for any amount of time, according to how tender you'd like it. It is slightly spicy, earthy, and sweeter when cooked longer. Use Western turnip as a substitute.

Katakuriko: A Japanese potato starch that is a great gluten-free alternative to flour or cornstarch when baking or deep-frying. Use cornstarch as a substitute.

Kobe Wagyu beef: Very high-end, tender, well-marbled beef from Wagyu cattle raised in Japan's Hyogo Prefecture in Kobe. Because it can be difficult to find, use any other well-marbled, tender beef, such as Prime or Choice Angus beef.

Kombu: Kelp that comes from shallower parts of the sea and is traditionally used in a dried, thick form to make dashi stock. Kombu should not be rinsed because the white powder on its surface is very flavorful.

Kurobuta pork: Pork from a Berkshire pig, Kurobuta is highly marbled and tends to have darker, more flavorful meat. If you can't find Kurobuta pork, use any other type of heritage-breed pork that will be similarly juicy and tender.

Layu: A Japanese variety of a Chinese chili oil commonly used as a condiment to add spice to any dish. It is typically made from a sesame oil infused with chopped chile pepper and paprika, giving it a reddish tint.

Lotus root (renkon): Visually appealing, the lotus root has tubular holes throughout, so when sliced, it is very attractive and decorative. Its taste and texture are similar to a water chestnut and its crunch holds up well in hot pot broths.

Maitake mushrooms: One of the most visually appealing Japanese mushrooms, maitake have ombre shades of brown and look like big, delicate flowers. They have a complex flavor that is fruity, earthy, and spicy. A dried variety can also be used by rehydrating in warm water. Use oyster mushrooms as a substitute.

Matcha: A finely ground green powder, rich in antioxidants, of different Japanese shade-grown green tea leaves. Unlike traditional teas that need to brew in tea bags that are then removed, matcha tea is dissolved in hot water.

Mirin: Sweetened rice wine, used to make teriyaki sauce, marinades, and dressings, and an all-purpose replacement for sugar. Although mirin contains low amounts of alcohol, it is safe for use in children's dishes as there is normally a very small amount added.

Miso: Fermented soybean paste made with cooked soybeans that have been fermented with koji (the edible fungus used to make miso and sake) and salt. For the purposes of this book, there are three varieties used: (1) shiro (white), with a milder flavor and slightly sweet, is often used in dressings and sauces; (2) aka (red), aged longer and saltier, is most commonly used in miso soup; (3) shinshu (yellow), with its medium flavor, is a combination of red and white, and can be used in condiments, soups, or marinades.

Mizuna: With its long stems and craggy leaves, mizuna looks almost like a weed. It's spicy but not overpowering and ideal in hot pots when you want an extra kick. It can be eaten raw or cooked. Use mustard greens or arugula as a substitute.

Mochi/mochi ovaletts: Pounded rice made of mochigome and formed into patties. It can be eaten as a dessert or used in savory dishes, soups, or by itself. Mochi ovaletts are small disks of mochi that tenderize when cooked and are used in hot pots to provide a texture variety and to soak up the broth.

Napa cabbage: Chinese cabbage commonly used in hot pots both in Japan and internationally. When cooked, this cabbage is tender and the lower ribs of the leaves retain their crunch.

Negi: Japanese green onion that is thicker, larger, and more flavorful than the Western scallion, or green onion. It tastes similar to a leek, but is sweeter when cooked.

Neri goma: A Japanese paste made from a puree of roasted sesame seeds. It is like tahini but has a stronger, richer sesame taste.

Nori: Dark purple, greenish paper-thin sheets of crispy seaweed that are available in large squares or shredded.

Ponzu: A citrus-based sauce commonly made with yuzu and a soy sauce base. It is typically used as a sauce for shabu-shabu but can also be used for marinating meat and as a dressing.

Sake: Japanese fermented rice wine. There are endless varieties that can be served hot or unfiltered and cold. When cooking, like anything, use one you would be happy to drink on its own.

Satsuma imo: A Japanese sweet potato with a dark purple skin and a creamy pale white interior from the Satsuma region of Japan. It is very sweet when baked, but, when used in hot pots and thinly sliced, it adds a nice balance to the savory cooking broths.

Shabu-shabu: Shabu-shabu is an onomatopoeia for the sound that food makes when you swish it back and forth in a boiling broth. Traditionally, this gentle waving of meat is done in boiling water and it is the ingredients that you swish around in the water that add flavor to it.

Shichimi togarashi: This blend consists of seven spices, normally various red peppers, black and white sesame seeds, poppy seeds, dried tangerine peel, nori or shiso, and sansho. It is used as a condiment and is a very popular addition to spice up hot pots.

Shiitake mushrooms: Rich, woody, and intense in flavor, these umami-filled mushrooms are the perfect choice for hot pots because they hold their own and impart flavor to any broth. The stems are very tough, so they are usually removed before use. Use rehydrated dried shiitake mushrooms as a substitute, but as they're stronger in flavor and aroma, you may want to use less.

Shime: Translated as "finish," this is the end-of-meal tradition for hot pots, when rice, noodles, or mochi are offered to complete the meal and satiate your guests. The hot pot broth, infused with the food offerings, will simmer down and concentrate into a highly flavorful liquid. The shime is added and absorbs this liquid, resulting in a very satisfying and delicious final course.

Shimeji mushrooms: These petite mushrooms are available in brown (buna) and white (ronfun) varieties. They grow in big clumps that you can trim and pull apart. They are mild in flavor and have a tender texture. Use enoki msuhrooms as a substitute.

Shio koji: An umami-rich condiment made from shio (or salt) and rice that is fermented with koji (the edible fungus used to make miso and sake).

Shirataki noodles: Made from the konjac yam, these noodles come in black and white varieties based on the type of yam. They come dried or stored in liquid, have relatively no flavor, and are gluten-free and low in carbs and calories. They are great for hot pots because they cook quickly and take on the flavor of any broth.

Shiso: Part of the mint family, shiso has a frilly leaf that makes an attractive addition to any hot pot. It has a plum-like flavor and can be eaten raw or cooked, or used as a condiment.

Shoyu: Japanese soy sauce, essential in all Japanese cooking. There are many varieties that can vary in flavor, aroma, and quality, so seek out ones that are naturally brewed without any additives. It has a milder flavor than Chinese soy sauce.

Shoyu koji: A savory condiment made from shoyu (Japanese soy sauce) and rice that is fermented with koji (the edible fungus used to make miso and sake).

Shungiku: This chrysanthemum leaf is a leafy green vegetable that is a little sour and bitter in taste. Their tough stems should be removed and they should only be lightly cooked to preserve their crispness. Use watercress as a substitute.

Soba noodles: Made from buckwheat flour or a combination of buckwheat and other flours, soba noodles are much thinner than udon and pair well with hot pots because they add a roasted, nutty flavor to the broth and cook quickly. They are also delightful and tender on their own and taste delicious when dipped in sauce.

Sukiyaki: A very traditional type of nabemono, or Japanese hot pot, that uses a mixture of sake, soy sauce, sugar, and mirin called *warishita* to flavor the dish. In Kansai-style sukiyaki, which is what is used for my recipes, the warishita is poured over the meat and vegetables.

Tofu: Made from pressed soybean curd and available in a variety of textures: (1) momen (firm tofu) has a firm texture and holds up well in hot pots, soups, and stews; (2) kinu (silken tofu) is more delicate in texture, with a smoother mouthfeel and cannot withstand much cooking, but is available in firmer varieties if you can find it; (3) aburaage (deep-fried tofu) is thinly sliced tofu that has been deep-fried until puffy and golden. It is a type of tofu not stored in water and is typically used for inari sushi, where the tofu pouch is opened and stuffed with seasoned rice. It is perfect in hot pots because it stays moist and spongy in texture even when soaked in broth; (4) yakudofu (grilled tofu) has been put under the broiler for a couple of minutes until it develops a speckled brown appearance. You can easily make this on your own or purchase it already broiled.

Udon noodles: Made from wheat flour, these noodles are thick and white and have a neutral flavor. Although they are available dry, the fresh or precooked varieties are preferred. Udon are perfect for the shime, or end-of-meal course, with hot pots, as they remain tender and their dense shape helps soak up any remaining broth.

Yuba: Made from the layers of skin forming on top of soy milk after it is simmered, yuba is available fresh or dried. If dried, soak it in water to rehydrate before use.

Yuzu: Not like a lemon or a lime, the yuzu has its own distinct flavor and a very fragrant peel. It's zesty but not overpowering and is the main ingredient in ponzu sauce.

INDEX

Page references in *italics* indicate images.

ACKNOWLEDGMENTS

Projects like this one take a small army to complete on so many levels, so I have many people that I'd like to show gratitude for.

First off, I'd like to thank my agent, Leslie Jonath, and the team at Race Point Publishing for continuing to guide me through the process of writing cookbooks and for helping to make this one really special.

Julia Vandenoever: You not only produced stunning photography, but also made shooting it easy and relaxed. Nicole Dominic, the style queen: You chose the most thoughtful serving ware and accompaniments to complement every dish in the best possible way. And Nancy Zamparelli: You are a food-stylist extraordinaire. It was so humbling to see you turn my dishes into masterpieces. I learned so much from all of you, and I'm super thankful that our time together allowed us to get to know each other on a personal level.

Julia Heffelfinger, cook, food writer, editor, and culinary producer: Hmmm, where do I start? So, not only do you have mad copyediting skillz, recipe-development knowledge, and cooking acumen, you're just fun to be with! Meeting with you every week meant my deadlines were sure to be met. You also provided me with a sense of calm, which helped me thoroughly enjoy the process. This book is better because of you.

I had the best recipe testers—Emily Teel, a freelance food writer, recipe editor, tester, and developer to name a few, and the team of SF Cooking School Alums, Nathalie Christian, Nicole Erickson, Anne Jung, and Danielle Kim: Thank you for showing me better ways of doing things and for giving me your time.

My recipe contributors and guest chefs, Emily Lai, Kiko Asaoka, my mom, Yvonne Magbee, and my cousin Emiko Ibaraki: It's so interesting and revealing to witness other people's creative processes and their use of ingredients. I love that all of your perspectives and ideas live within this book. These recipes are among some of my favorites, and I can't wait for people to learn from your lifetimes of experience. My cousin Emiko was also my go-to for advice on the correct way to do things from a first-generation Japanese perspective.

My wonderful family, my husband Dave, my daughters, Maggie and Ellie, and my son, Ryan: For Dave, who encouraged and supported me throughout and always offered to get last-minute groceries with a smile on his way home from work, even though that was probably the last thing he wanted to do. For my kids, who put up with having "mean-mommy" come out when I was feeling like I was lacking the creative juices to make one more hot pot seem original and when those deadlines felt like too much for me to bear. You guys let me hole up in my office writing recipes and headnotes while you took care of yourselves—all in patient anticipation of the day the book would be done and you'd get your mom back. Thank you, my family, for sitting at the table multiple times a week for hot pot meals, giving me the most positive feedback and encouragement, and continuing to affirm that this would all be worth it. I love you so much and couldn't have done this without you.

ABOUT THE AUTHOR

AMY KIMOTO-KAHN is a *yonsei*, a fourth-generation Japanese-American, wife and mom of three, who lives in Boulder, Colorado. She is a student of her families' long history of cooking and continues to share her favorite recipes on her blog, *easypeasyjapanesey*. She also works part time as a personal chef and is the author of *Simply Ramen: A Complete Course in Preparing Ramen Meals at Home*. When she isn't cooking, she runs her own marketing firm, Fat Duck Consulting, that she founded in 2008. You can find her sharing new culinary experiences and foodie travels on her Instagram: *e.p.j.*